Essays From The Couch

Volume III: Realities

2013

WILLIAM S. HOROWITZ, M.D.

This collection is dedicated to the memory of
Peggy Sr., Mimi, and Rob, all of whom left before their
time and are sorely missed.

Acknowledgments

I am totally in debt to my helpful wife, Gloria Jean, for sustaining me, enabling me to write. Too, our talks have often provided the stimulation for new ideas to develop. My son Nicholas, Philip Bronner, M.D. and Kelly Talbot have all shepherded this work into print, for which I am most grateful. My family, colleagues, friends and patients have all played a significant role in addition. I conceive of these collected works as my legacy and tribute to my and Gloria's families.

Mission Statement:

Both the 19th Century Freud and his 20th Century disciple confirm the wisdom of their historic predecessor: "And the truth shall set you free."
But that emancipation is not easily achieved, for adult man still wrestles with the shackles of ancient indoctrination, presented by the clerics as guidance but effecting instead his obedience. The transmission of values and conduct is valuable; the powerful inhibition of man thinking for himself is what is crippling.
The sharing of his unique mental life with an understanding companion re-establishes that original nurturing bond with another which releases the inherent growth of the self and its own thinking, an actual, not metaphorical, re-birth.

Table of Contents

ACCOUNTABILITY

William S. Horowitz, M.D.
June 4th, 2013
Thanks to Gloria, again !

That television master of ceremonies, the foremost expositor of *fairness*....."*Still Number One !*"....opines that violence in the Negro and Hispanic communities is the scourge of our society, and solicits from his expert guests a monotonous litany of causes, including the predictable family breakdown, fatherlessness, racial stigma, and overall bad luck.

They all agree in synchronized tongue-clucking tsk-tsking "What a Shame !" that white sympathy should be afforded these minority unfortunates for their *unfair lot in life* as the cause of all their troubles, whilst simultaneously supplying to them the perfect excuse for their atrocious behavior.

You can count on the fingers of one hand the Negro writers who would strongly disagree with that sentiment (including Cosby, Sowell, Williams, West and Carson), who don't hesitate to confront the black community with its very own responsibility for its bad behavior and, hence, its only path to redemption, but the white society persists in giving them a pass which only guarantees its persistence. Most of the last century has seen NO change in those troubling statistics of violence and incarceration, nor the groups' lock-step voting for the Democratic philosophy which espouses faux (non-existent) aid to those groups.

A previous essay noted our peculiar historic tolerance of savages in our society, ascribing it at bottom to a sense of religious ennoblement through *self-sacrifice or martyrdom*. As such, it is highly valued and hence persistent, and perhaps even enviable ! The Moslems display photographs of their bursting cemeteries of young self-sacrificing martyrs....not so different, come to think of it, from our *very own* repositories of dead soldiers scattered all over the globe !

We have saved the world in the process, true, but is *that our assigned mission?* By whom, and for what? An intelligent Arab named Nader has inveighed against Corporate America and its military/industrial complex for this tradition, and rightly identified its money-making value, but he doesn't touch the hot-button issues of Moslem martyrdom or cant in his analysis. It is a familiar accusation of American *greed* by the espousers of the four-wife privilege. (A Viennese Jew of the Victorian age taught us the principle of psychological *projection.*)

Lincoln wrestled with the thorny issue of what to do with the freed slaves....include them, send them back, resettle them.... finally granting them full citizenship....which the American society demurred with for over a century. In a similar vein but to a lesser extent, we also granted unlimited immigration with our empty space and *Anchor Baby* laws, to which again the "people" are having their objections. Are we as a nation lacking self-protection ? Are we suicidal ? That is a grievous suggestion, but not so irrelevant these days of Limbaugh's silent *COUP DE ETAT.*

A FATHER'S PLEA

William S. Horowitz, M.D.
January 28, 2013

The U. S. Air Force adopted as its motto: "AIM HIGH" ! During WW II, Admiral King advised: "DO THE BEST YOU CAN WITH WHAT YOU HAVE". Congressman John Vasconcellos started the "SELF-ESTEEM" movement in California. Thomas Jefferson enumerated the value of Liberty and the Pursuit of Happiness, which professor Steven Allison says taking personal responsibility for and pursuit thereof provides the earned benefits and SELF-SATISFACTION of working in the capitalist system, and accounts for its singular success amongst all the historic societies.

That was then; this is now. Are we considering PRIDE ? We are told on Sundays that it is a sin, or at least too much of it, and needs to be countered with the virtue of HUMILITY. Our current leader-in-chief, imported from a totally alien ethos, decries AMERICAN EXCEPTIONALISM as arrogance, and that it should give way to the leveling of all other societies, being a major cause of our national troubles. There is a popular movement in America today to devalue the recognition of achievement in school, sports, and competition in general. Earlier this past century Ayn Rand's philosophy of INDI-VIDUALISM was devalued as SELFISHNESS.

Half our current population is on the dole, with its obvious erosion of self-esteem. Rampant corruption in the governmental ranks, not to mention rampant civil incivility with the population shooting themselves wholesale. What in God's name has happened to our morality or morale?

There, I said it, the naughty word, now passe. One doesn't have to follow any specific religious affiliation, or even be a non-believer altogether, to understand that there are forces in nature, Mother Nature and Father Time being good exemplifications of those forces, that SUPERCEDE man's individual powers and reach, that lay down the unbreakable facts of existence, that provide the guidelines, the rules, the morality.

"I will do as I please", say the rebellious ones, "and indulge my fancies." What the good Fathers say is: "Don't, you won't like yourself.......aim high, do and be your very best, remember your old pride. don't let them degrade you !"

A NEW APPEARANCE OF AN OLD DEFENSE AGAINST OBJECT-LOSS

William S. Horowitz, M.D.
January 25th, 2013

Loss of crucially important love-objects has been identified "forever" in the psychiatric literature as an enduring trauma to the developing individual. Multiply that by multiple repetitions of the losses and you have a major chronic psychological trauma affecting both development and functioning, a kind of emotionally battered person, what we label nowadays as PTSD.

Without expanding at this point with a description of its various symptoms, let us focus instead on the stages of reaction to death itself. The immediate one is shock, then grief, then more protracted mourning as the absence is remembered and repetitively experienced. A mood of sadness, despair, anergy, pessimism, mistrust, futility, weakened will to live may ensue and persist for surprisingly long periods, and it is here the consideration of killing of others and the self enters.

With time and therapy this chain of reactions may wane, or it may not. What could account for that, the absence of relief and persistence of this chronic "mood"? Here, Sigmund comes to the rescue, both with his discovery of the unconscious, and his naming of the then-extant symptom cluster, along with Charcot, HYSTERIA.

What we, or I, see, is the suggestion that the subject has unconsciously IDENTIFIED with his dead relative, and is struggling to cope with its effects. That is to say, literally. that he/she is already dead, and yes, possibly already buried, together again. Not in awareness, remember, but the flags show themselves everywhere.

First, the negatives or absences: there may be a feeling of nonexistence, absence of self, no feelings, ideas, words to say, things to do, total focus on others. It is a step beyond anhedonia, it is

NOTHINGNESS. Acting (going through the motions; the source of AS-IF?). There may be a preoccupation with death and burial phenomena, or with the anticipation of death and its date of appearance, suspicious hypochondria of immanent (fatal) illness, actual plans/requests for one's own funeral, phobic avoidance of attending them, fear of and avoidance of inactivity (going to the couch).

Then there are positive effects: a universally expanded interest and display of CREATIVITY in all its varied forms: art, new ideas, discoveries, re-DOing, re-NEWing, novel ways of doing old things (recipes, re-decorating), cultivating new growth out of dead wood (gardening), seeking and enjoying activities of others, keeping moving.

Then there may be neutral or regressive thoughts, about "the good old days" before the trauma, the perfection of childhood, idealism, the absence of fear in "not knowing" (what lies ahead), with a subsequent intellectual inhibition or faux stupidity, the comforting blanket of ignorance.

To further confuse the picture, all these "flags" may co-exist right alongside the healthy functioning ego, making the diagnostician's head spin. That's me, until today, when I realized the subject felt falsely dead and alive simultaneously. And then I have to wonder: WHY?

Are our civilian and military populations OVERLY- traumatized compared to earlier times? The movies, TV, "games" all say YES ! Were families more intact and hence more healing and comforting back then? Probably so ! Do multiple mass killings BY CHILDREN reflect an anxious society? Absolutely NO DOUBT ! In certain places and times, military suicides EXCEED losses by warfare. We have a political "leader" bent on the destruction and transformation of our nation. Do we not FEEL this?

Does death-preoccupation betoken a dying society ? Or possibly are we witness to an apparent rash of outbreaks resulting from the morbid feature of hysteria, its contagious-ness, or tendency for its subjects to identify with each other (ala the Salem Witches). Or is it merely the re-set of another Aztec wheel of time? To the extent that we as an American society anticipate or already experience its immanent loss, are we already "in bed" with that, inclined to passively accept it without a struggle?

"ALL MEN ARE CREATED EQUAL"...?

William S. Horowitz, M.D.
March 7, 2013

This is the most difficult essay I have attempted, having agonized over how to get my idea across effectively and fairly. To give you some background on me which may shed light on my perspective as author, I am an 88 yr. old retired psychoanalyst of the old school, classically trained, who has written two books of clinical studies and philosophical essays, now with 50 new essays ready to publish with the tentative title of "Realities". THIS is the subject of my preoccupation that I wish to clarify and then teach.

Since the topic concerns the American society, I must add that I am first generation, my parents from Mittel Europe with 3rd and 8th grade educations, my father a poor peddler with a former lost wife and child, now married to a well-to-do crippled wife, my mother, with an older sister and two large extended families, 1/2 practicing Jews, 1/2 renunciating faith in favor of a strong "American" identification. I grew up in a rich neighborhood while my family was on near-welfare, was offered a full scholarship to a prestigious University in my junior year but prohibited because "needed" at home; had two tours of duty with the armed forces, one of which sent me to medical school. Married now 4 times with 2 children, enjoying the support of a loving wife which allows me to keep going and write.

This title is the credo of a democracy, and the American one to be sure. But...is it true? In what sense? It seems to mean that politically, no one has an inherent power over another, and all are fit to participate in the governing of their society. But, prior to participating, the members have to exist, and many do not survive the womb, infant mortality, and the first year of life. Those were not equal (to the rest). Power over their fellow man? The infant nursery demonstrates a rich variety of temperaments, the later school years an even richer variety of health, stature, intelligence, social class, wealth, and privilege that belies the title of equals.

But I originally characterized it as political, and even here there are restrictions on voting and office-holding, historically racial plus land-holding and poll tax ones, within my lifetime gender restrictions, even currently age and good citizenship ones....not equal politically.

If we can agree so far, what else does the motto communicate, or infer? The idea that America is the land of opportunity, for anyone can become anything he wishes and works for. Without a doubt this apothegm has drawn millions of huddled masses to our shores to participate in THE DREAM. Hollywood, the world-wide manufacturer of fantasy, has recognized its market's location is right here ! Does this mean the American public are fantasists? Well, they enjoy it, famously and remuneratively!

Much of the old world lives from hand-to-mouth, but Is there not something between a hard-scrabble existence and make-believe? How about sobriety? Would you say our people, especially the young ones, who drop out of school in large numbers, idolize trivial television entertainers, utilize sensorium-modifying drugs freely, engage in here-to-fore unheard-of acts of violence and sexual predation, and live on the earnings of their serious neighbors...are sober? Are REAL?

Not that further evidence is needed, but note that in the most basic of functions, our society is NOT reproducing itself (at a 2.1 rate for two parents). Then there is the minor matter of them twice electing a NON-American to be a NON-President, who threatens to transform and dictate, which we seem powerless to stop.

The easy explanation is that our culture lets them, indulges them, even supplies the wherewithal. The harder idea to contemplate is that the indulgence came first, while raising them, so that character, ability to navigate and succeed in a competitive world, the building of strength and fiber was never promoted, and the evident laxity in their adult lives was an after-effect of their weakness toward life, unable to face it.

Reading a history of nineteenth and twentieth century Europe, and particularly Germany's growing interest in developing a super-race, parallel to the appearance of dictatorships in diverse societies around the world, all strongly suggest a temper of unease and fear among nations in those times. Their view of idealized America as something to be wondered at...aroused in this observer for the first time the question whether was the same anomie at work here in forming own beloved culture....resulting in something NOT REAL ?

Does the very idealism of its founding guarantee unreachable goals and hence eventual failure, often via equally inauthentic values? Some historic societies have prevailed for thousands of years; the predictable duration of "democracies" has been 250 years over many different eras.

Life is hard...but can be rewarding. There is no achievement without effort. You are not entitled, nor have it coming.. (Your) time is not endless. Love can conquer a helluva lot, but not all. These are some of the nuts and bolts of life to be learned, what we call the verities; they help make a structure, which will serve you. Your life will be what you make of it.

ARE THE NEGROES A FAILED SOCIETY?

William S. Horowitz, M.D.
July 27, 2013

That is a very big question, not readily posed in polite society. And it is a dangerous question to be posed in polite society. So why pose it? In my last days on earth, I am compelled to consider the unthinkable but obvious, so far blindly denied by all who would not see.

An astute social observer passing himself off as a self-taught radio commentator recently quoted a new "study" finding that the recent American immigrants, legal and not, seem to be following the path of our previous nation fillers in following historical patterns of assimilation into our *"Melting Pot" All except for the Negroes!*

All of those immigrants take any work they can find, many recent invaders from south of the border can be found hanging around street corners waiting to be hired for day-work at a pittance *just to be working and earning something!* Of course the better educated and socialized do more. The Negro experience was different, having been captured in Africa, sold here as slaves to southern farmers, and finally freed by a magnanimous nation after a bitter civil war a century and half ago (in which they participated in fighting for their own freedom).

Little does that picture of energetic self-preservation and participation in the young society's citizenship resemble what we witness today, which is almost the exact opposite. There are exemplars of culture, education, invention, and industry to be found in the group to be sure, not to be gainsaid, but the overwhelming numbers of the Negro race have failed to adopt the institutions of our society, to assimilate, to join with their "rescuers" in joint venture, in their language and values, or to exert *any effort at all.* Families are disintegrating without fathers, babies are born almost exclusively without wedlock, children drop out of school, crime and imprisonment is the usual fate of youth, killings of their own and whites are commonplace, and a characteristic para-culture is practiced.

They have converted themselves from contributors to takers, living off the compassionate guilt of a Christian nation. Six writers, astute Negro social critics, contribute the bulk of moral leadership and group criticism, plus a sprinkling of political vanguards during their tenure here. But so far, things continue to deteriorate in the Negro society, with no sign of real improvement. Street (civil) war between the colors is a very real possibility in the future. And we feed their grievance by indulging them, mistakenly excusing them for their behavior.

So what, one might ask? Animal and plant species have come and gone down through the ages, and so have human political entities, whole societies, in the course of history. That the failure of a sub-culture of America can occur should be no surprise to a student of civilization. The question is whether it is a realistic possibility and reflects the facts, or is a phantasied construct of reassuring denial.

Reflect that our world has gone through a century of decimating war, eliminating a huge enough fraction of our young manhood (of *all societies)* that foreign workers had to be imported to replace the various labor forces, *and the world-wide human reproduction rate dropped below replacement !* (With the notable exception of the Moslems with their policy of reproductive conquest.)The problem we are witnessing is therefore UNIVERSAL, NOT sub-cultural ! We are *all* in the same boat, sinking ! All of us humans, white and otherwise, who, except for the Chinese, representing perhaps the oldest extant civilization on earth, seem to be coming into flower.

So, the bottom line, as they say, is whether *human civilization* all together is in decline, with possibly a nascent replacement "in the wings". That indeed will spin your head to contemplate. Meanwhile, "Have a Nice Day."

"AS-IF" PERSONALITY: A CLINICAL CAUTION

William S. Horowitz, M.D.
June 17, 2010

In 1934, Dr. Helene Deutsch first described unanalyzable patients who appear treatable but fail to engage in the therapeutic process. She described the subjects as appearing perfectly normal but somehow inauthentic, aping behavior from their environment, acting rather than being. You can familiarize yourself with her original description by Googling the title, which won't be repeated here.

She offered no dynamic explanation in this brief introduction, though a colleague Dr. Masud Kahn proposed a super-ego defect and she wondered if there was an underlying schizoid syndrome. Having attempted to analyze two patients resembling her description, I believe I have uncovered a dynamic operative in those cases.

Frank X, a forty-ish married graphic artist was employed as a color designer and coordinator in industry, while producing serigraphs as his hobby. Why he came for help I cannot recall, but he seemed genuinely motivated to cooperate in a 5-time/week classical analysis. This was pursued by an eager young candidate with furor therapeuticus, alas, to no avail.

He associated (and I interpreted) according to the recipe, and was perfectly satisfied to go on endlessly, although the interpreter came to realize that he, himself, was not, for in total agreement with Deutsch realized nothing was happening as treatment wore on. No insights, no change in behavior, no discoveries, no deepening, no development, and no dissatisfaction with that state of affairs.

To amplify, he belonged to a normal-appearing social circle, one member of which knew me and referred him. I don't think he was regarded as odd in this circle, i.e. was socially adept. He loved his wife and repeatedly described how they spent the whole night as

19

"spoons", nested together as curved utensils in the silverware drawer. Two other features of his functioning remain in my memory: his artistic prints were colorful, elaborate architectural constructions absolutely devoid of life, warmth, symbolic content, or evoking of emotion in the viewer. And the second, his favorite language noun was "form", modified by a another describing the type of form, e.g. life-form, circle-form, building-form, etc. These were not actual entities in reality, but representations of them. Deutsch does posit "A lack of cathexis in their objects" in these patients.

Realizing my interventions were having no effect whilst he continued to offer me material to elicit my interest, I determined that his aim was exactly that, to keep me interested. He was, by so doing, keeping me and holding me closer. This, I believe, is the functioning dynamic at work, controlling the analyst as the young infant holds and controls his mother. It is the seeking and preservation of intimacy of a primordial kind, the achievement of which afforded him all the satisfaction he sought.

The young analyst, frustrated at his seemingly meaningless efforts, stopped responding to his patient's presented clues and so tried silence as a therapeutic technique. Five weeks went by with absolutely no change in his behavior, and so, when he realized he lost control of me, he left. No regrets, no recriminations, no emotion of any kind. I am not especially delighted with my experiment, but at least I now feel I understand it. But I do have regrets at not having helped him.

The posited "lack of cathexis of their objects" means their "significant others" are not real to them, not incorporated object representations with feelings and meaning attached, not residua of actual historical relationships but "forms" of them, as the patient would say (as in "this is an allusion of an umbrella-form"). This incorporation of abiding internal objects normally ensues from meaningful relationships with separate real people, a phase following the primitive controlling/merging relationship with mother which the patient is trying to recapture, and typically is enhanced with the loss of the real relationship (as separating and moving beyond).

This "as-if" symptomatology suggests the original relationship with mother was never successfully achieved and graduated from.

The possible whys are manifold: early loss of her, inability of her's to bond with her infant or to wean him from it once established, some unknown limitation of his, who knows? So the individual physically grows up acting with unreal representations of real people, acting inauthentic himself, a poseur so to speak.

Whether free associations from the couch, or the conversations from the chair, both seem real enough as the therapist tries to empathize with what is being communicated so as to understand it and respond. But the talk is not shared communication but vocal acts, serving as provocation of the therapist's reactions, primary process we call it. Not only are people not real to him, but words likewise are not, often merely aping of what the therapist said. It is certainly possible that gradations of these qualities can be found in different individuals, more or less so to speak, but the underlying meaninglessness is unmistakable and arouses a counter-transference reaction in the therapist of at first boredom, then frustration, then resentment at being fooled.

What about subjects that adopt acting as a profession, can they be successfully analyzed? They give a typical history of dropping out of high school to join the stage, possibly a clue to their educability and use of manipulation of their audience; years of attempts with them have left me no clear answer. Other narcissistic personalities of divers stripes, gypsies, con-artists, other dissimulators are likewise problematic. The British Object-Relations School of Melanie Klein, Winnicott, et al addresses these early stages of functioning utilizing such concepts as symbiosis, projective identification, false self and others claim possible therapeutic effect; of this I cannot attest.

On a superficial level, these subjects could be seen as a caricature of adolescents making trial identifications of admired models before consolidating into an organized identity (and growing up)... hence may benefit more from mentoring than psychiatric "therapy". The analyst, sensing this patient's actual need and responding to his/ her typical seductiveness may find himself abandoning his "blank screen" and offering himself as a real object, yet another counter-transference hazard. Far from a problematic analytic lapse, however, the recognition of the role of the "real" therapist has given rise to a whole school of theory and technique by Bettleheim in Chicago called "The Corrective Emotional Experience", and in Los Angeles and New York by men like Greenson, arguing the therapeutic value of the real relationship vs. the transference one.

BONDAGE

William S. Horowitz, M. D.
May 25, 2013
Thanks to Gloria, again !

Not only are the human genders uniquely different, but the nature of their relationships are also distinctly their own. They are so different, in fact, that the more one studies them, the more miraculous their eventual getting together appears. A previous study showed that the constitutions of the sexes are _not_ symmetrically balanced, the male starting out his formative years in an enraptured relationship to a female several decades his senior in life experience, startling fact enough to boggle your assumptions.

To take the simpler of the two cases first, the human male appears to be on a straightforward developmental progression from start to finish, marked by total _dependence_ on the female, from infancy to dotage, with nary a relieving variation on the way. To be sure, the object of his dependency may change, but the attitude to her remains monotonously the same: _neediness_. And she is programmed to fulfill that need, physically, emotionally, gratifyingly to both.

That he may be prone to adopt the defense of _denial_ does absolutely nothing to modify this state of affairs; you can detect this defense by his early adoption of _contempt_ for his mother, not to mention his later amassing of endless supplies during his productive life. What is being described here is his underlying _relation to his objects_, a separate dimension of his functioning not incompatible with Freud's classical stages of psychosexual development, and not precluding his maturing into a potent providing and protecting male. It has been called _anaclitic, or leaning_. However, throughout life at times of stress, such as his wife's childbirths or the waning of his powers in middle-age, his "_ego_" or sense of self-worth remains vulnerable and requiring bolstering, often via the love of a new woman.

The female, on the other hand, is _locked into_ her attachment to him by her physiology, constituting a kind of _bondage_ during her reproductive years. This state expands to include both the mate and the children produced, though the latter tends to outlast the former for most of her life. It is only when the family has been successfully generated does the bond to her mate weaken, whereupon she becomes tired of care-taking and needy herself, often looking to herself, other females, and her grown children for companionship and care. The diagnosis of _Tired Mother_ Syndrome is no cliché. The characteristics of _passivity, loyalty, sense of duty, receptivity,_ and _felt-inferiority_ spring from this state of bondage.

None of this is incompatible with classical stages of psychosexual development, but in the case of an attractive juvenile unwilling to undertake the heavy responsibilities of family formation, a popular outcome is the attraction to the performing theater and finding of a "sugar daddy" for support and companionship. Her underlying _relation to her objects_ has been called _narcissistic_, but her _"ego"_ is not rendered thereby as especially vulnerable since it is based on actual accomplishment and the continuation of her relations with her children. Thus we see the typical male dalliances with assorted females during his beloved wife's parturitions, and the post-childbearing wife's desiring some care-taking herself after reducing her duties.

Men and women are uniquely fitted to fulfill their social roles in human society: what happens in modern times when they don't? Can a woman forego child-bearing, a man marriage? Of course. These are _instinctive_ patterns which can yield to conscious choice, though there may be a price to be paid for doing so. In the case of the cleric's foregoing of connubial bliss, posited by some philosophers as his device to enforce chastity in his flock, one could say he enjoys actually an expanded family by so doing.

What is the effect of the male child not knowing his beloved mother as a person like himself? Does she remain, and all females remain, _unreal,_ subject to idealization and its opposite, perhaps accounting for irrational displays of love and/or aggression toward her, enhanced rivalry, inability to accord her appropriate social value, greater comfort in relating to those of his own kind? These are not trivial questions.

By all measures, the female appears to be the stronger of the two, at total variance to her perceived "inferiority". How can this be? Is it simply the immature girl child's misinterpretation (and her family's) of the absence of any of the anatomical equipment possessed by her mother, father and brothers that leads to this mistaken impression of genital inferiority? They say *"first impressions"* are the strongest, nicht wahr? Note how quickly that sense is dispelled upon the emergence of the breasts in puberty and her discovery of her new-found powers over boys. However, many adult women carry a residual feeling of "flaw" in some part of their anatomy unable to be "fixed".

What effect is the destruction of the products of conception on the female's womanliness? That would seem to depend on other unknown factors; but for sure, her unconscious carries a sense of *guilt,* correctly interpreting the abortion as *murder.* To the extent that society's reproductive rate has fallen below replacement, we see the importation of foreign peoples into heretofore stable societies having an entirely predictable heterogeneous mixing of populations and decline of community values. *Not* an insignificant consequence. Is it too much to hope that serious puzzling societal problems have their roots in quite simple sources leading to eventual correction?

CHILD'S PLAY

William S. Horowitz, M.D.
March 14, 2013

Watching out the kitchen window at her little children at play, our modern mother is unknowingly repeating eons-old behavior practiced by the females of the animal kingdom as they raise their young. One could say the newbies are building their physical and psychological infrastructure upon which, in time, their adult skills will be built. The rudimentary beginnings have been selected and preserved by the biological races as having survival value, and hence are far from meaningless activity.

The human boys are exercising their strength, fighting, conquering fear by risky feats, and taking initiative toward imaginary foes. The girls are having carefree joyous fun exercising their bodies in rhythm, and trying on grown-up shoes, hats, and lip-stick. All of this substantially duplicating the lion mother with her cubs (of both genders) as she watches and protects them from menaces in the surround including their father !

If play is the non-serious development of useful adult skills, can there be disturbances in the process? Is the adolescent yearling lion cub yet ready to protect itself from enemies, fend for food, survive? What is the effect of poverty or war-time disruption of normal peaceful conditions on the development of brave men and charming women in our societies ? We can imagine. But we know what results in our own contemporary culture when the children spend undue amounts of their development time on television or hand-held toys: the men can become non-self-sustaining earners, defenders of their country, or founders of new families, and the women may remain single and childless. From lack of play? You rule it out as a non-factor !

One of the skills learned when children played with each other was interpersonal relations, not how to be by oneself. The currently popular misnamed "Social Media" serves less as an adjunctive communication enhancer than a vehicle for individual exhibitionism. To add yet a further deterrent, contemporary liberal society has decreed that boy's pointing "finger guns" is incorrect, which, along with other gender-specific behaviors is to be punished in the name of sexual uniformity. What is the product of all this interference? It could be classed as A-social training..

Earlier we referred to the danger animal fathers pose to their species' offspring, being well-known to eliminate them in favor of siring their own. Human fathers are also well-known to not relate to infants until they acquire more familiar abilities. Does this possibly hint that little infants are not the "apple of their eye", are in fact rivals for the female's attention? Might that have something to do with the current rife incidence of sexual predation of children by men, and also our male-dominated legislators' reluctance to protect them by law? Speculation, I know...but it makes one wonder.

I am continually impressed with the fun-loving "silliness" of young girls, and the contrasting seriousness of young boys. Has Mother Nature arranged this for a reason? What might that be? Does it serve a useful leavening of their spirits for the couple's eventual foray into adult life?

For sure it is an irresistible attraction to the male: try to imagine courting a young woman who is "no fun"!

Play is a rehearsal of whet is to come, and what will be needed to cope with that future. As such, it is part and parcel of the supplies a youngster needs to survive and thrive, which also includes formal education, loving parents, and enough wherewithal to navigate in modern society. Like what's in the bottle, that's a nutritious formula.

COLONIES

William S. Horowitz, M.D.

August 26, 2013

With Gloria

I have no special knowledge to impart, I wasn't there, but I want to plant a seed as my wife taught me by offering my musings from intuition. This is for *thinking,* not *feelings.* It claims no *factual or political* basis, only *biological,* with no intent to offend.

The starting point was asking "What were the Negroes like BEFORE being taken slave?" Was its African population like the passive lay-abouts of today, the savage brutal youngsters on TV, or the rare highly intelligent, creative, empathetic geniuses at our universities? One would guess the former because the whole fabulously asset-rich continent remained undeveloped for centuries before the European nations captured chunks of it for exploitation. And among those assets collected, probably seduced rather than vanquished, were whole tribes of people possibly sold on the idea of being given something of value in a foreign land. They were NOT vanquished warriors (think Roman centurions) as was the age-old custom, judging by a generally passive acceptance of their lot, given function, and survivability. Rebellion or escape was a later development.

The Northern African desert territory which was the site of that European colonization was eventually won over by the Arabs, developed into nations to be sure but of no great note, just as the whole continent before them. The advent of the Dutch in South Africa developed the only independent productive nation into modern times on the continent.

The American native Indians had their tribes already organized into "nations" and developed a successful way of life with nature, which after capture by us and re-colonization into reservations did spectacularly poorly until discovering an industry, at which they are becoming equally spectacularly successful.

America, too, originally was a colony developed for exploitation of its natural resources (cotton, land, wealth). After throwing off the shackles of being occupied and successfully burgeoning in our independence, we in time imported foreign labor to harvest those assets since we had so few workers of our own. Did that make *us* a colonial power, too? And thus join the rest of Europe in the inevitable deterioration of our economies and societies because of it?

Is *intrinsic* development generative of growth and success, whilst imported help degrades our own neglected strengths? Does homogeneity of a population make for progress and development, or only stability (cf. Switzerland)? Does heterogeneity or mixing of peoples make for IN-stability and eventual DIS-solution? The *democratic* form of government has an historic short shelf-life, 200-259 years; *why*? Ralph Peters opines that "people" don't like to mix, preferring their own kind. Modern college campuses, once segregated, then mixed racially *and* genderly, now are witnessing a return to their former state.

Jews may illuminate history again. They do not constitute a genetically pure group (per Schlomo Sands) but a religion and culture which has survived passively but productively by virtue of enclaves in various host countries. Perhaps *they* could be thought of as quasi-colonies, often taking root. Their passive acceptance of marching to their demise in Germany demonstrates their loss of sustaining resistance qua dispersed colonies, whilst the militant productive character of the newly *nationalized* Israelis (Sabras) is the envy of all emergent *and* older states. Has this been predictive of what could happen if domestic Negro colonies are attenuated, whilst as an organized nation could survive and thrive? Liberia was one of Lincoln's such suggestions; it utterly failed, however. A test case?.

As the world turns and its societies age, its peoples self-segregate into like-minded enclaves, colonies if you will, in the "mother" state that harbored them, progressively expressing frustration at not being supported enough and often making a nuisance of themselves to the host country. What have we learned about *individual* development? That there comes a time when the family and offspring will do better apart...so we say to them "You are big enough to look after your own needs, take responsibility for yourself, enter the world of grown-ups and do your negotiations with them". Are colonies like developing teenagers with a natural maturational development....no different than other biological forms? Should we cut off the allowance and wish them "Good Luck, you are on your own"?

One has the impression *our* contemporary society is beyond recovery to its former state. What then is its fate? Culture wars between groups of like-minded peoples...an eventual winner....a new form? Old societies have come and gone, and there is no intrinsic reason for us to be an exception. Nor are we "entitled" to our former traditional life. So, sit back, contemplate, and join me in hopefully observing a differential maturation *into independence.* We've had ours, now its time for *our* dependents foreign and domestic, *all of them.* Maybe the best "foreign Aid" is leaving them alone, to experience the real world, not the womb.

EMPTY WORDS

William S. Horowitz, M.D.
September 28, 2012

In 1934 Helene Deutsch M.D. called our attention to a new patient phenomenon which she called the AS-IF Personality . She described their unanalyzability but offered no true dynamic explanation. They seemed normal in all respects, physically cooperated in the process of free association, but nothing happened in the therapeutic process!

I herewith present my understanding for your consideration, as well as a new label.

All of us have witnessed, nay, experienced the fascination a new human infant arouses in us. The intriguing thing is to speculate that this same infant, increasingly as he matures, experiences his random perceptions of his surrounding real world as fascinating, too.

It is as though this stage of development is marked by a quality of heightened perception, by both the viewer as well as the viewed. Sounds super-natural, doesn't it? But in our adult real world we have a name for something, an ineffable quality, which inures to certain people who fascinate us: charisma. Is this a later recognition, a re-edition, of the same thing?

What is the psychological medium that is being heightened? It is the perceptual function of attention. Our heightened attention is drawn to the infant even as his is drawn to the multifarious objects in his surround. To make a leap to a somewhat (months) later development, the infant realizes he can capture the attention of his attendants, can manipulate them into action, can control them.

(Earlier with merely sounds, later by learned effective words, which are not offered messages from one person to another but rather vocal acts which have known effects on the listener.)

This constitutes a definitive operation, function, phase, call it what you like, in the infant's first year of experience in this world: the manipulation of others' attention to control and hold them.

We loosely call it the young (narcissist) drawing our attention, but it is much more complicated, powerful, and effective that that implies. It is a fixed phase of psychological functioning of the infant, tails off in ensuing years of development, hopefully to disappear in the well-functioning adult ...BUT IS FIXATED IN THE PROBAND WE CALL "AS-IF" OR CHARISMATIC CHARACTER.

In the psychoanalytic situation, absolutely everything the patient produces is an object of the analyst's scrutiny. It is a perfect medium for our subject to operate in, and he will, endlessly, for years even, without producing anything meaningful. That leads to the analyst's belated recognition that "nothing is happening" in the therapeutic situation and giving it up. When the proband realizes he has lost his effect and control, he leaves, his sole gratification having been eliminated. This is exactly the same as when the political observer says he cannot respond to Obama's mouthings because there is NOTHING in them. Our essay, therefore, has wide and profound implications, far beyond those of our parochial profession.

Such persons become fluent in the use of language, as you can imagine, as well social and vocational activities that work to elicit attention, among which advertisers, actors, and politicians are well represented. THE most egregious exemplars are the centuries' infamous dictators. Rare, yes, but among us. To this I wish to make every sentient citizen aware. Let us call it provisionally "Pretend Talk".

FISCAL ESSAY

William S. Horowitz, M.D.
5 January 2013
Gloria's Modest Proposal

Rush Limbaugh says the politicians are just buying votes with their largesse. As astute and sensitive as he is about the reality of political psychology, I believe he is WRONG !

There is another dynamic at work, related but even more explanatory functioning here, which is even more important to understand...and it will not be delivered by any of our "gurus".

I believe politics to be the art of exercising power over others. It is therefore the natural bailiwick of government, which in turn is the natural attraction to MEN, who enjoy the accumulation of power for it renders them BIG, what we call an EGO-TRIP. To have endless pots of money to dispense to those wanting, to carry the heavy responsibility of government office, to preside over a whole nation let alone have at hand the hegemony of Western Civilization...this is the desideratum of all possible perfections. ! To give it up ? IMPOSSIBLE !!

You don't have to search for an explanation of governmental lockjaw in arcane political theory, it is an everyday common dynamic: mens' EGO. !

How do we recognize an ego-trip? By the emphasis on EGO or SELF. These are people who delight in talking about themselves. How do we recognize its absence? By the presence of self-effacement, humility, focus on the OTHER: the people, the national situation, universal values. We call such a person a STATESMAN, and we search desperately to find one (...in another human sphere we call him a genuine MESSIAH.)

It would be nice to have one of those around to help solve our "Fiscal" problem, but until he comes along, my wife has a simple suggestion: How about a WOMAN who already handles success-fully most families' money, and who has no over-riding need to be BIG; who In fact, by nature delights in finding a bargain and SAV-ING money. How about that !!!

We have had some successful women in government, to be sure, but some of them have fallen victim to "liberation" and model them-selves after men. I am referring here to feminine women who can chair a legislative session AND save money at the very same time (without chewing gum). Don't get me wrong, men are also o.k. in my book, particularly those who are secure about it and have no need to go on trips.

FREETHINKER

William S. Horowitz, M.D.

July 6, 2013

Dedicated to the Memory of Margaret Mae Hamilton and her Mothering of Gloria Jean Horowitz

What is a *"Free Thinker"* ? One who ascribes to no fixed school of thought, philosophy, system of belief, or assorted creed or known vocation. That is, has not been indoctrinated or identified specifically with familiar patterns of mentation peculiar to everyday *callings*, or has rebelled out of membership in one. It is formless, airy, nonsubstantial, can seem like *"nothing"*. And, in fact, the free thinker can feel like *she is nothing*, can confuse herself with having no substance or identity. The free thinker may indeed believe *she IS nothing*.

We ask the young "What do they want to BE?". They answer, "What do you mean, I already AM !" What do we mean when we ask that question? Not that they are formless, which indeed they are, but what sort of existence do they imagine for themselves? Do they then choose a way to BE ? Yes, out of a cafeteria of options they are witness to growing up, in their family, their society, their schools, they finally make a choice, provisional and later final, of what they want to *be*. So, the school demands: "What's your Major"?

Hopefully in institutions of "higher learning" they are exposed to varieties of thought espoused down through history so that they are taught, not *what* to think, but *how* to think. Sad to say, that aim is usually failed, and the highly educated one usually emerges indoctrinated and politicized.

What happens when the subject is NOT pressed into a specific form, but left to develop like a creature in the wild, a wild flower so to speak. This is the case of the neglected child, "abandoned to nature", a sadly repeated experience too often in our society. Such a child does grow up feeling like *nothing, as expected*. What follows predictably, besides a major impairment of *ego or self,* is a frantic search for *something* to identify with, to feel like *somebody, not* different. Gangs and radical politics attract these eager adherents (not to mention organized religions)..

But there are exceptional parents who *deliberately* avoid orienting their child to their own personal perspective in order to pass down the gift of *freedom* they feel was denied them. They *want* their child to be a free thinker, in spite of its own *insecurity* cost. Some deliberately spare the child the parochial familial religious affiliation for this purpose, although in practice this *freedom* is granted or ceded only in adolescence: "Now you can choose for yourself".

Does free thinking lead to confusion rather than clarity? Not usually but it can. Does it lead to atheism? Not necessarily, though accused of it. Does it lead to radical extremism and chaos? This is a fear induced by those captured already and envious of it. There is no downside to freedom of thought, except for feeling "different" and un-identified.....a major deterrent, perhaps, but a small price to pay for the rewards. What are they? Inventiveness, creativity, animatedness, liveliness, energy, curiosity, accomplishment, leadership and THE KEY to appreciating and adding to the "culture" in all its variegated, velvety richness.

They don't *FIT IN* frictionless with others, for all they have really known of people's ways are their own, and they *WANT it,* like an only child. Two are explosive !

HE IS DEAF, DUMB, AND BLIND ABOUT HER.

William S. Horowitz, M.D.
3 February, 2013
Thanks, Gloria

Why do men treat women as they do, idealizing them at one time, totally ignoring and neglecting them at another, venting physical rage on them not rarely, having NO understanding of how they feel and think? The answer, I believe, lies in the first relationship with her, his mother, as he is loved and nurtured through his very first years. A veritable "love affair" exists between them, so powerful it echoes throughout their lifetimes, well into his old age and decline.

The clue to understanding various phenomena which I hope to illustrate to you.... the clue recently conceptualized is that he does NOT perceive or conceive of her as a PERSON. She is something else, sometimes a phantasy, sometimes nothing, often as a re-edition of himself, but not as an individual human person with all its attributes. Why IS that?

The "relationship" starts out as a merged entity of ONE, so there are no separate individuals. When in the course of development there occurs a dawning separation of "selves", the two are so totally mismatched in size, capacity, ability, and need that NO similarity or comparability exists...she knows him, he is clueless about her. He is an amazed new person discovering the world for the first time; she is a grown adult human already several decades experienced. It is a powerful emotional affair between two totally mismatched selves.

This asymmetry alone accounts for the problematic "relationship between the sexes" familiar to us all. He is ignorant (of her), she is knowing (about him). He doesn't know how she feels, what she is thinking, what she values and desires, what she fears, what she takes pleasure and satisfaction in. Does the (little) child understand the adult? Does the mother know her child? She reads him like a book !

Now that that point is made, let's move on to its effects:

1) Men are enthralled with the discovery of a new adult love, and will move "heaven and earth" to (re-)capture and possess it. She is typically personified as "the girl next door" (?familiarity?).

2) With the eventual waning of the thrall, he is ever susceptible to its recovery in a new passion, ready to sacrifice his now-established family, wife and children, for the magnetic draw of the new, without a second thought about how THEY feel about it.

3) If his passion is not reciprocated in full, a ready rage reaction ensues, with "no holds barred" expressions of physical destruction. It is unthinking infantile rage, a temper tantrum now of adult proportions.

4) Throughout life the asymmetry persists: HE protects his dear Mom, HE offers his seat to the lady, HE asks for her hand in marriage, He gives his name to her, in his declining years He reverts to his original need for her care-taking, He dies before her as the newcomer and dependent in the partnership.

5) Fascinating to wonder whether the woman's secondary status in society is an historical effect of man's ambivalent (over and under) valuation of her, accompanied by his prideful denial of his own dependency on her, and further reinforced by her (motherly) indulgence and pride of him, as well as her characteristic receptivity and reconciliation with tradition (experienced as "normal").

6) The impetus for the female liberation movement lies here, obviously, but not necessarily the direction it has taken. In an effort to raise their status and restore their unrecognized integrity, too often the political claim of "equality" is transformed into "sameness" (with men) resulting in a correspondingly tortured appearance of traits of masculinity, and the loss of femininity. "Equality" is the vote, the charge card; "sameness" or identity has no place in human affairs (only animal clones), which are typified by, if nothing else, DIFFERENCE. The explanation of our political taboo against this recognition is a whole new topic.

HEY! I'M A GIRL!!

William S. Horowitz, M.D.
December 24, 2012
(To and from Gloria)

I became aware that I regarded my wife as a person, as another person like myself, requiring a separate step to remind myself (or be reminded) that she was of a different gender. This would happen after some repartee in which I spoke (offensively to her)_ "like I was living in a barracks". Although I have spent time exclusively in the company of men, sports teams and the military and the like, I was raised with a sister and went through a co-ed school system. Her experience, oppositely, was fatherless. Did I demonstrate a lack of empathy for her, and/or she for me?

What is the function of the universal tiny white hair bow on the head of the little girl infant sitting up to be admired? Is it adornment, or is it something else... an identification of her gender which would be otherwise not evident? What is the function of all the conspicuous jewelry the adult female displays.... is that adornment, or is that the wearer enjoying the feeling of being feminine?

(i.e. does she herself require reinforcing her identity?) Why this special need to identify the female?

It has been thus in all of man kind. Ah, there's the answer.... in the language. It was totally genderless until recent times, until under the advocacy of the women's' movement when "he/she" was introduced (or "he" eliminated). Humans were formerly lumped together as one species. Does this reflect how humans thought about themselves, without regard for gender, before the modern elaboration? We, as a species, do not further specify when speaking of other (animal) species: we talk of them as a whole type, lions and tigers. What is the point?

Men and women mate, for the most part, and in doing so expect to collaborate in raising a family together.... but famously, working together is fraught with miscommunication, leading to the "battle of the sexes" and the belated recognition that "Men are from Mars". Do they not speak the same language? It only seems so. So, their perceptions of each other, their words, their feeling for the other's feelings, their empathy, may be as distinctively different as their hormones and their torsos. And yet, they expect their mating will be smooth and intermeshed.

Animals (our biological reference) represent varying types of mating: some are opportunistic, some are seasonal, some are permanent. Human societies have their cultures, and those cultures have their customs and habits which undergo changes, some times within our very own life-time. (We used to have large families with plenty of exposure to the opposite sibs.) Is the mating of the human, and their consequent reproductive rate, in jeopardy, after vast demographic changes including unfamiliarity ? One would be hard pressed to deny the possibility. The American society is almost alone among the world's nations in reproducing itself.

IN THE BEGINNING...

William S. Horowitz, M.D.
August 18, 2013

Exploring ever more deeply to understand man's mind, we turn to the ancient sources who were actually there to remember and update us on how it all started.

They tell us our first human parents, Adam and Eve, felt the need to cover their animal nakedness, perhaps in part to distinguish themselves from those wild creatures. Thus they invented the *fig leaf*, to clothe that remnant of animal kinship as though to dissociate themselves from that heritage. Did that do it? Well, hardly, for down through the millennia of advancing development. mankind continued to struggle with this primordial emotion, even within each generation : *SHAME*. The cover does indeed obscure what lies beneath ; the leaf itself persists. *That* is what we struggle to understand in human behavior.

Firstly, how do we experience shame in our daily life? The original object of shame is the *body* itself, if it is malformed, misshapen, with disproportionate development, even fully normal and beautiful but a gender perceived as *inferior,* showing budding secondary sexual signs, or with parts not matching then-current standards. (Ask *any* contemporary woman the "size" of her "deficient" body part and she will say "five pounds". Amazing !)

Second as a frequent source of shame is the *family*, either as an entity in itself or compared to the family at large of all the relatives. Like with the body, when it seems "not up to snuff" to the ideal, or in comparison with others that appear better, it can be a powerful and persistent and deep-going hidden embarrassment. Factor in a drinker, divorce, name-change, poverty, conviction, foreigner, aberrant life-style or *anything different* from the milieu and the attendant shame is multiplied, especially in the growing school child acutely needing to "fit in". And the child's own misbehavior likewise contributes to the family's disgrace.

What do we employ as cover, the fig leaf? Here we find as multitudinous a variety as the human mind is capable of inventing. So much so that the choice of this defense may be the major determinant of the character of the developing human. First order defense is *denial,* probably universally practiced. Second order is turning shame into its opposite, *pride.* This in turn can be magnified to any desired degree, rendering in extreme cases the distorted phenomenon of the super-saver, written about in Imelda Marcos and Liberace and any of countless multi-billionaires. Paradoxically, some historic evil-doers like Soros also boast of their dark "accomplishments", and even be lauded by society for them. This illuminates the common practice of ordinary citizens morphing into career criminals, repeating and exaggerating their transgressions into a source of prideful superiority to cover their nakedness.

So we have denial and turning a feeling into its opposite. But its not necessary to *feel* at all, for one can *"couldn't care less"* or not at all, making one's existence a meaningless pseudo-life. And its also not necessary *to know,* the second of two omnibus defenses (or figs) adaptable to all situations.

The latter defense is wrapping oneself in the comfort of ignorance, a pseudo-stupidity not at all incompatible with high intelligence and often found with it. You can not know what's happening, or if do, what it signifies. You can complain modern life is too complicated, and yearn and search for the *simple life,* turn to nature, live outdoors or in a commune, or make children or creatures your companions.

The former fig is erecting a pseudo-life by means of *acting.* Early psychoanalysts identified such unreal personalities as "As-If", who essentially manipulated people's reacting to them, controlling the audience's attention whilst avoiding genuine interactions with them. They *appear* to be regular humans but are merely imitating them, playing a role just as they usually end up doing, performing on the stage or at your door as the consummate professional salesman. They are pseudo-real, but without the travail of emotions of their own.

Sensing appropriately the realistic impotence and ignorance of his newborn state (notably soothed with his hypomanic "love affair" with the world), the developing child is incentivised to continue to overcome these deficiencies by growing up and doing right. That is, he feels bad but wants to feel good. So, shame provides an important spur to him to overcome, not avoid.

"I WANT MY RIGHTS !"

William S. Horowitz, M.D.
March 12, 2013

What are they ? Life, Liberty, and the Pursuit of Happiness said our Founding Fathers. How can he or they deliver them ? By inspiration, not by law: If everyone believes in them, perhaps they will come about by consensus. So they are a credo, an objective, a goal, a promise, an inspiration, a spiritual declaration, a political fiction, whether or not written down in actual words.

Claimants will claim they are God-given rights. How do they know, and who told them ? Who is this voice on high who says, "You are entitled" ? Sounds awfully much like located in the claimant's own head. Other claimants will cite our founding papers as the source, as though written-down words can control citizens' behavior. Is our Constitution a set of laws to be enforced, or a guide to the making of enforceable laws ? Remember, they were written on paper, not stone.

Well, then, says yet another claimant, they WERE enacted into enforceable law from the Civil Rights era, a standard of "equal" treatment from man to fellow man. True enough, they embraced a code of fair conduct between the individuals of a diverse society: a black man cannot be excluded from a white man's bailiwick by law, par exemplo. But he can be by private club rules: the sorority can admit or refuse anyone it likes.

What in the older society was held as obligation TO that society, e.g. military service, is now felt as obligation FROM it, i.e., to provide housing, food, spending money, unlimited immigration, and telephones. A "civil right" ? Hardly. It was a naked unprincipled political bribe by the progressive LEFT administration to gain adherents and political power. When the character of the American society is finally "fundamentally transformed" with its color changed, the Democrat party will have much to answer for....but historically they have NEVER been called to account so far.

So, we have a code of conduct between diverse individuals, some of which is concretized into enforceable law, but that is a far cry from a general license to claim entitlement to ANYTHING one wants. What used to be "wish" is now "need", then "right" to have it. THAT is how the "civil" rights have been morphed into general license, privilege, entitlement, indulgence, and "spoiling". We have been CONNED. Our society, and sorry to say our government, are now busy extending and ablating limits to what we used to call sexual perversions. What do YOU have coming? Stake your claim; it's your civil RIGHT.

The counter-forces in our society, the "conservative" silent majority, the Republican party, have an equally sorry history of protecting our actual rights to good government, good values, a good society, and that failure has yet to be fully explicated. The thesis proposed by this observer is that the idealism inherent in our democracy has its own built-in flaw (the absence of an effective mechanism for removal), that very perfection which cannot be reached and perforce must fail. The older, experienced conflicting political factions in pre-war (1800 & 1900's) western Europe during the formation of nations from principalities and then dictatorships, looked at American democracy with wonder as a "Pretentious Sham", i.e., looking good but not working (only 250 years, remember?). Does THAT give you a new perspective on the country you grew up in, one which is in process of changing into something else?

"I'LL TAKE THE HIGH ROAD..."

William S. Horowitz, M.D.
January 28, 2013

The U. S. Air Force adopted as its motto: "AIM HIGH" ! During WW II, Admiral King advised: "DO THE BEST YOU CAN WITH WHAT YOU HAVE". Congressman John Vasconcellos started the "SELF-ESTEEM" movement in California. Thomas Jefferson enumerated the value of Liberty and the Pursuit of Happiness, which professor Steven Allison says taking personal responsibility for and pursuit thereof provides the earned benefits and SELF-SATISFACTION of working in the capitalist system.

Are we discussing PRIDE ? We are told on Sundays that is a sin, or at least too much of it, and needs to be balanced with the virtue of HUMILITY. Our current Leader-in-Chief, imported from a totally alien ethos, decries AMERICAN EXCEPTIONALISM as arrogance, and that it should give way to the leveling of all other societies, being a major cause of our national troubles. There is a popular movement in America today to devalue the recognition of achievement in school, sports, and competition in general. Earlier this past century Ayn Rand's philosophy of INDIVIDUALISM was devalued as SELFISHNESS.

Half our current population is on the dole, with its obvious erosion of self-esteem. Rampant corruption in the governmental ranks, not to mention rampant civil incivility with the population shooting themselves wholesale. What in God's name has happened to our morality or morale?

There, I said it, the naughty word, now passe and to be eliminated. We are turning GOD-LESS. One doesn't have to follow any specific religious affiliation, or be a non-believer altogether, to understand that there are forces in nature, Mother Nature and Father Time are good exemplifications of those forces, that SUPERCEDE man's individual powers and latitudes, that lay down the irresistible rules of existence, that provide the guidelines, the rules, the morality.

"I will do as I please" say the rebellious ones, and indulge any fancy coming my way. What the good Fathers say is: "Don't, it affects you badly, you won't like yourself.......AIM HIGH, DO AND BE YOUR VERY BEST, MAINTAIN YOUR PRIDE !"

JUDGMENT

William S. Horowitz, M.D.
August 14, 2013

It's misuse is usually ascribed to organic injury to the front of the front of the brain, the *pre*-frontal cortex, the location of the brain's executive functions of which this may be the highest. BUT, this function is vulnerable to psychodynamic (IN-organic) misuse also, perhaps even more frequently. Perhaps the location also hints at the history of its evolution, being the latest addition to human development.

"Lower" forms certainly also have this function, lest they would be unable to reconcile their needs and evaluation of their environment to satisfy those needs (and could not then survive). Perhaps the exercise of human judgment entails those very same functions but at a more sophisticated level.

Let us consider those functions. First in priority would be memory, for without it, no comparison with past events would be possible, nor an appreciation of the passage of time. With it, a nexus is established, of time, place, and person (identity of), against which background the current situation can be compared. Being ori ented, we call it. Without knowing "what's going on" changes in the situation cannot be evaluated. And that in turn requires previous evaluations having been made. Here we see the exercise of cumulative functions, each leaning on or borrowing from the previous. A 3-dimensional picture is constructed.

With an understanding of its present situation and potential (imagined) changes being contemplated, an evaluation is possible, to its *liking or not*. This would be the first appearance of judgment. But note the appearance of a new function, that of *imagination*, regarding possible future changes (or *consequences*). One has to *anticipate* (past memory) what the imagined activity will effect. That requires giving it some *thought*...that requires taking some *time*....that requires *delaying* a decision and consequent action. Those are *final* steps in the whole process of executing the brain's other functions, not immediate ones. Some people regularly mentally *rehearse* their anticipated actions before carrying them out, to test those effects safely. That's *prudent.*

Are there influences on the exercise of these functions? The pressure of need (say, hunger) versus satisfaction, the pressure of time (say, opportunity) versus its absence (say, future opportunities), the pressure of current events (say, already on trial for the same infraction) versus a clean record, the presence of a stress-less hiatus in activity in which to make a judgment...and so on. Age, length and variety of life experience, past learning and self-correction, accumulated "wisdom" so to speak are all additional factors. And there are many more if one digs more deeply. such as motivation to be *right.*

What's the point of this exegesis? Perhaps to emphasize the complexity of exercising judgment judiciously rather than as an impetuous child demanding its way. To illustrate, when responding to a social appointment, say a dinner, job interview, or board meeting, would it be IN-judicious to arrive 5 minutes *early*, before perhaps the arrangements had not been completed nor the private conversations readied for sampling, compared to 5 minutes *late* when your host was fully prepared for your arrival? We call that "fashionable" or exercising *tact,* a useful, nay necessary skill in successful human relations not exercised by the *klutz, loser, or career* misfit. The possible motivation for a life-long practice of these behaviors are too numerous to detail here, but a general carelessness, not caring nor feeling the need to care might suffice.

JUSTICE

William S. Horowitz, M.D.
August 3, 2013

The mechanical T.V. spokesman announces today's news : "Picked up this morning is this [unshaven 35 yr old] wearing an electronic ankle bracelet because of overcrowded jail, out on bail awaiting trial for raping a woman, apprehended after raping another woman."

I can see it now with my only slightly beclouded glasses : after a many- week to a year wait, he will be tried, convicted, and sentenced to 10, 20, (maybe even 100 years in the case of undue indignation) back into the jammed jail as his "punishment".

Would some sympathetic soul out there *pleeze* enlighten me.... WHERE IS THE JUSTICE ? Is there some satisfaction forthcoming to the TWO victims ? Not likely, more likely *bitterness* at the indifference of her fellow man to her. How about the other good women witnessing this as they hide their daughters behind their skirts. Shouts of pleasure? Not likely. How about the citizens at large in this society ? Are they feeling accomplished at the jails brimming over, never wondering what attracts so many to this system of "justice"? I wondered, but no more; it has utterly failed as a deterrent, maybe even functions as an attractant, lowering the cost of criminal activity and thereby raising the reward.

To the judges, believing they are performing an important social function, as their calendar now stretches into *years ahead?* Not apparently, as their office hours stretch all the way from mid-morning to mid-afternoon, leaving ample time for "consideration, advisement", and decision-making. To the lawyers? Well, it's a living. As satisfying or not as it may be, there is no denying they perform a social function something like the street-sweepers of the 1800-'s. Is that JUSTICE? Or house-cleaning of the mess in its absence?

In the "olden days" on the frontier of this young nation (I have a *long* memory), they didn't have overcrowded jails, or communities

53

over-run with rapists and murderers. When they caught a relatively ordinary criminal stealing someone else's horse, they held a "trial" at the nearest tall tree and strung him up, and dry-washed their hands in satisfaction afterwards. To my un-modern, un-sophisticated, un-sympathetic mind, THAT WAS JUSTICE !

What, who have changed this? The so-called "bleeding hearts? Our reaching for *ideals?* Our losing touch with the hard feel of *reality?* An admired English tradition of good manners ? Christian "tolerance" ? Our "getting by", complacency, successful survival ? Is that success to be our undoing? What a damned shame if that is the case.

Indian Braves learn in the school of Mother Nature for that is what they have to deal with, having little or nothing beclouding between them. Now, *we* have thermostatically heated homes, but has Nature changed, specifically *human* nature? Obviously not. Are some people out to capture us, control us, "scalp" us? Does the weather care if it floods us, dries our fields, terrifies us with its storms? Do we think we have conquered Nature with our inventions and products? When we tell Jose that what he is doing is "against the law" (another one of our inventions), do we think he is listening, understanding, caring what another is thinking?

Now it is no longer necessary for each of us to grow our own corn, but possessing heaps of it loose in open public display should alert us to the fact that residents of neighboring communities may not have any and covet what we do....(which even the Brave would understand). Simple realities are quite sufficient to adjudge and dispose of *criminal* (asocial) acts. Gradations of heinous (totally unacceptable) behavior serve absolutely no purpose but legal employment and psychological curiosity. It would be perfectly efficient to have a jury trial to adjudge whether the act, including *all* degrees of killing, were justified or not in the opinion of the jury of peers ("would *they* do it?). *That* would produce "justice" : quick, cheap, and deterrent punishment. Culpability is no arcane legalism but a simple human judgment. Our legal system, and its community sponsor, could take a lesson from any ordinary business, athletic team, or military unit about prompt elimination of members who don't fit in.

To the extent we pursue actual practices of IN-justice, to that extent we reap an UN-just society, such as we are suffering today.

LOOK AT ME !!
(IT'S ABSENCE CAN BE LETHAL)

William S. Horowitz, M.D.
December 18, 2012

When the human egg and sperm meet and "fertilize", they merge into one, the genetic strands unify themselves, then twist together as a random exchange of genes called amphimixis takes place. Then the single fertilized cell separates into two permanent composites of genes and proceed to cell multiplication. This process is usually successful and will lead with development into a viable human being. But it is not always successful, with the result that the zygotes fail to develop, or do so but erratically and eventuate into a fetus that spontaneously aborts, is still-born, or develops into a flawed new-born with a truncated life-span. Not all chance combinations of genes are automatically life-supporting, and Nature usually eliminates them.

In the animal kingdom, we know that a new-born which does not interact with its mother cannot survive. A human infant who, on the very first day, refuses to make eye-contact with its mother is gravely flawed, exhibiting the earliest signs of a-sociability, by whatever name we wish to call it. However we try to salvage such a human, its destiny is marked and we, the observing society, must reconcile ourselves to that reality.

There are varying degrees of expression of this non-relating to one's fellows, of course, but the quality of the defect is no different in the hater, simple loner, the "autistic", the stealthy bomber, or the political war-monger, starvation meister, or outright mass-murderer, of which our past century had an abundance. That may have been the bloodiest century in history... if anyone really knows.

There are also degrees of resistance in us to recognizing the gravity of anti-social manifestations, with our usual soft-hearted avoidance of hard-nosed policies (which have given rise to eugenics and the "master race"). What is so difficult about recognizing that people who do not like their fellow social beings are killers, in mind and action? (Haters wipe you out by not looking at you, symbolically eliminating you... an everyday observation. Diplomats who want to break-off relations refuse to recognize you. Ex-lovers are not seeing their former paramours anymore.) Seems like common sense, eh? (We are not discussing criminals, also called anti-socials, whose antipathy is not to the whole human race.)

Several factors may play a role in our not comprehending this. Narcissism, or self-love cannot imagine not being loved, also called hostility; religious mythology, which values everyone as a creature of God's perfection; a mental health system preoccupied with "therapy"; a legal system proscribing predictive action; a fuzzy juvenile political philosophy of "equality, fairness and rights" which cannot differentiate; and sincere human compassion being pained is thus avoided. And so it goes. So, as usual, there are reasons why things are as they are; that doesn't mean, though, that they can't change. Perhaps in some future world, we will have come to recognize the potential lethality of a-socials early on.

LOVE

William S. Horowitz, M.D.
July 30, 2013

What is it? We think we know, but do we? First-hand? Have we experienced it; do we know it when its there?

It's a *feeling*; we have a love *for,* and can feel loved *by*... another. It is *good, warm, comforting, drawing close, touching.* It is *not* bad, cold, distancing, or even neutral.

How do you know if you have had it? If you haven't, you might *well not.* If you've had it, you usually do. A man wants to love, *needs* to give love, feels foiled if not allowed, feels fulfilled if may. A woman wants *to be* loved, to receive it, feels fulfilled if forthcoming. A man *satisfies* his loving urge by giving, the woman by receiving. This coordinated action is what creates new life in humans.

Still haven't defined it, beyond being an emotion and an urge to action. Is it necessary and sufficient in human relationships? NOT AT ALL! Loveless side-by-side activities are common in many activities of life, including sad-to-say family life. We *assume* it where it may not exist at all, because we are young and don't know better, and because we *wish* it, and because *we* have it. Perhaps it is a saving grace, or self-preservation, which inures us to its absence. We are trying to come to grips here with what may be a major bug-a-boo of human existence: NOT being loved (wanted, belonging, appreciated, valued, yes, touched).

Paradoxically, we can experience each of those feelings toward another *without* loving, so *that* element is separate and distinctive. And *ineffable?* If we can't put our (mental) finger on it, how do we know if its there? Is it possible we don't....that we can progress through life never having experienced it and not knowing that? Are people we know products of love-less groups we call families, raised together AS-IF they really belonged together? Can a baby be conceived in the absence of love? EVERY DAY!

Perhaps the problem is not recognizing love, but its *absence*. Perhaps our "better nature" blinds us to that particular pain. So that we seek love, and maybe think we have it, when in fact we exist all our lives without it. Whoever promised us a rose-garden?

So, perhaps an individual can exist and even develop in a family nexus that lacks particular focus on him, taking him "for granted" as they go about their other business, and perhaps this eventuality is more common that imagined, maybe even "the rule". Such a person is a full-bodied person, but *not* experiencing membership in a family of mutually concerned relatives. He would then be feeling like an orphan, an *observer* rather than participant with others, likely then seeking to share his existence in other people's lives, to borrow a family so to speak. How? By actually spending inordinate time at friends' homes growing up (running with a gang), accumulating and cultivating groups of friends like assembling a family, reading about others' lives, marrying into a family, making a family (getting pregnant), or inserting oneself into others' lives as trusted friend, counselor, or classic psychoanalyst meeting with a coterie of patients daily for a period of *years*!

Would someone already having a real family (love) do this?

MAD DOG

William S. Horowitz, M.D.
December 28th, 2012

Rudy Giuliani is credited with instituting the "Broken Windows" policy in New York City to begin the Herculean task of reducing crime there. It was a recognition that "cleaning up" minor manifestations of lawlessness gets the message out to the major transgressors that the neglect, the tolerance, the indifference to their incivility was no more. AND IT WORKED!

Today it is reported that a black "man" was apprehended after setting fire to a homeless woman sitting on a park bench. Also reported by our "news media" that a 17 yr. old (white?) youth in Texas calmly shot his mother and sisters before flatly describing what he had done to the 911 operator he chatted with "while not knowing why he did it." Rare events? Maybe, for this one single day after Christmas only. These reports are coming in bunches these days. An epidemic?

Ask yourself what YOU would have done if YOU were the apprehending officer in the first case. Try him, treat him? I know what I would have done, and I can taste it in my mouth: I would have SHOT HIM DEAD on the spot as a vicious dangerous animal who had NO PLACE in human society ! And I would not be tortured afterwards with doubts, regrets, or apologies.

If you are squirming with moral discomfort now, I don't want you as dog catcher, police officer, preacher, therapist, columnist, or public policy official, let alone citizen, in MY town. I don't want you because you are confused, thought- less, irresponsible, and cowardly. YOU and those like you are enablers and abettors of the evils that threaten to overwhelm us. Did you know that Singapore has a zero tolerance for drug dealers in their community? They execute them !

What is this twisted logic that tolerates this savagery in our midst? In an earlier essay I traced the history of commingling with uncivilized peoples by our missionary types who seemed ennobled by self-sacrifice (as in providing the dinner in the big boiling pot). We, as the perhaps most highly developed Western society, have a sad history of welcoming the uncivilized into our midst. Are YOU feeling a better soul with what is happening to us? Do you actually know a minister of the gospel who does?

If we want our civilization to survive and prosper, we must follow Mother Nature and ELIMINATE all who are not adapted to it. This is not cruelty or bias or intolerance or un-Godliness, it is reality !

My motto: GET USED TO IT !

MARRIAGE: An absolving view

William S. Horowitz, M.D.
June 12, 2013

What an unbelievably complex arrangement between two people setting out to establish a family this is. It seems so simple and straight-forward, but can be fraught with a life-long sense of guilt and shame when it fails. Let us try to examine why this should be.

Is there something wrong with a marriage of _only_ 25 years, which produced healthy children and supported two adult productive lives before it was dissolved? And if it was ultimately given up in favor of a 40 year liaison by one of the partners, is that evidence of fault?

How do we make these _judgments?_ We have what we read in the Bible and other ancient histories; we have a more contemporary tradition from our particular culture and grandparents to compare; we hear our clerics measuring how to think about these issues in their metrics of morality and righteousness; and I suppose we are well aware of what our relatives and current neighbors are doing. What we _don't_ think about when someone "_catches our eye_", because "_love is blind_", are the myriad of compatible factors which must go into such a prospective working partnership.

To name only a "few": age, life experience and degree of maturity achieved from it, size, strength, health, interpersonal comfort, social class, education, I.Q., vocation, geography, expectations, values, aspirations, perseverance, gender roles, the society we live in, comfort with children, etc., need I really go on? It is _much too much_ to think about, and we don't....until later, much later, when the disparate factors begin to rub.

Maybe traditional marriage will not exist in the future....our millennials seem to be telling us so. And perhaps the apparent current weakness in family formation, with its lack of producing the next generation worldwide, will make the issue irrelevant ultimately. But, whatever is in store for us, perhaps we should recognize and honor what our society has produced so far, and what we individually have risked and accomplished, and forget about those who haven't even tried !

We are discussing only one of the various expressions of _EROS_ in the human, _all_ of which are a beautiful derivative of our instincts.... _not something to feel ashamed of or embarrassed by._ We have loved ! This natural behavior, however conventionally or heretically expressed, has been co-opted by both the religious and civic communities, the one enforcing vows before God, the other establishing a legal contract with stated obligations. The latter, codifying the post-contract obligations of the stronger towards the weaker, are a justified source of feelings of failure, if not worse, if not observed. The former, falling short of some ideal "eternal" promise, are not of the same weight, and perhaps supply the puzzling sense of shame to the less-than-perfect union.

Two normal civilians deciding to do their lives together, but not achieving the ultimate silver or gold award, is no failure. We were only commissioned to _GO FORTH AND MULTIPLY._

MEANING II

William S. Horowitz, M.D.
November 23, 2012

What do you mean (by that)? We say it everyday and know its general significance, but trying to define it is another matter. We have many substitutes for it, such as the aforementioned significance, relevance, something we care about...but its essence escapes us. Why belabor or explore the subject anyway? Because as life goes on, this quality of existence seems to be dissipating, taking with it the emotion of caring. Is that Mother Nature's way of preparing us? Do other living (and dying) creatures experience it? They do seem to drop off into increasing bouts of sleep, which could be described as not caring.

Meaning seems to be adjunctive, connected to or evoking another mental function, such as remembering, feeling, or understanding. What means something to us is what moves us in some way. We feel because of it. (The detective's clue which has no connection is unmoving and irrelevant.)

What is the human's meaning of life? Ultimately that is a philosophical or religious question, but in immediate terms, humans experience it. The meaning IS the experience, the living of it. Are we then talking about another synonym...reality? They are not quite equivalent, but related: reality has meaning, and vice versa.

Cathexis is a psychoanalytic term for psychic energy: when a mental representation or idea is cathected, it is experienced; if decathected, it is no longer. One could say cathexis gives meaning to something in the mind. Helene Deutsch says," AS-IF characters don't cathect their objects", meaning the mental representations of the people in their lives have no reality. (A recent reading suggests she may have mistaken the trait for a characterological rather than a biological one, with entirely different significance. This author, Nassir Ghaemi, "A First-Rate Madness", is studying the relation of mental illness to leadership, in all the recent examples. His thesis is "normality" fails in leadership, unstable or ill ones are the ones who succeed.)

What does it signify that we cannot define a word but know its meaning? Is the meaning not in the language but in the experience itself? Inside the human, not in the word symbol? We seem to be saying that meaning is intimately connected to experiencing life, and that anything that evokes that feeling of meaning is REAL to us.

I don't know our understanding of this, or any other term, has been advanced, but perhaps deepened and mysterified.

MOTHERHOOD

William S. Horowitz, M.D.
February 5, 2013

Musing on the recently discovered non-personhood perception of the mother in the eyes of both her (now-grown) husband plus both her boy and girl children, combined with and reinforced by her own voluntary sacrifice of it, is it any wonder that she feels devalued and looks at men as models to be envied? Who would ever want to be a mother under these circumstances? This being the meat of the mother's self-regard, why then do they do it?

Maternal "instinct" ?.... what is that? Do we know what mixture of genes, hormones, historical tradition, personal experience, identification with her mother, love of her husband, all together constitute it? Do we have to know". Doesn't it suffice to acknowledge that mothering is a universal and eternal "fact of biological life"? Yes, BUT... there seems to be less of it going on throughout the world. If it's so permanent a part of human equipment, how can that be?

Population studies amongst lower forms shows overcrowding lowers the reproductive rate. We know the globe as a whole is not over populated, but it does seem to be undergoing a generalized upheaval of traditional social and political arrangements. Could we be witnessing insecurity and fear affecting partnering and reproduction? A likely supposition. Might there be other, less familiar, forces at work, such as the running down of the Aztec generational time clock, extra-terrestrial influences, the exhaustion of the natural biological life of this planet?

No one knows, of course... but the appearance of the apparent violation of hardened "facts of life" leads to these outre wonderings.

We alone, unique America, seem to be rescuing the phenomenon of mothering but just barely...but then, being "the hope of the world" is our familiar burden. And it is the female's burden almost alone. Preparing for her role in reproduction detracts from several days of every month for three plus decades, almost a year of gestation requires special care, delivering her product is extremely painful and dangerous, followed by two decades of exquisite attention to the needs of another. The male's making of seed, on the other hand, is silent and unfelt, his supplying of it a pure pleasure, rarely it can be dispensed with altogether, and his enlisting as helper in cultivating their product is entirely discretionary, though we require he pay for it. The burden of reproduction, then, is entirely one-sided, unfairly borne, but compensated for by her unmatchable supply of love and satisfaction, stronger nature and consequential importance.

We, all of us children of mothers, remain highly ambivalent about her, elevating her to sainthood or demoting her as the root source of all our troubles. Again, who would volunteer for that "hot" seat? But they do. Some by choice, some not, but in serving the essential requirement of our existence, we owe her EVERYTHING.

This is yet another manifestation of the principle of one-ness, not bilaterality, in biology (Queen bee + drones).

MY SOAPBOX

William S. Horowitz, M.D.
June 25, 2013

Do you share my offense when the "journalist" on the radio, TV, or newspaper re-re-reiterates "Former U.S. President Harry S. Truman" ? Who the _hell_ does he think he's talking to...Rip Van Winkle ? If you ask him, likely he will say, "That's proper reportage form as taught at the Columbia School of Journalism". Yes, I say, that's where it comes from, but it's NOT proper journalism form, it is _deliberate manipulative political propaganda_, NOT by the "left, progressives, radicals, or democrats", all the euphemisms invented for their disguise, but by the _ANTI-AMERICANS_ in our country ! There, I've said it !

Call it if you will a "vast conspiracy theory", one of their favorite depreciating snubs, but I think I understand now why and how it happens that the vast majority of American citizens seem clueless, apathetic, disempowered of their "voice of the people", plain dumb, "low-information", divested of their "exceptionalism, when in fact they are a potent, loyal, intelligent, latent counterforce to the anti-Americans. This is no accident, nor puzzling erroneous stat. It is the deliberate result of those anti-Americans at work in our society for perhaps generations. There are no legitimate political parties here worthy of their names, left or right, Dems or Conservatives, only Anti-Americans and Pro-Americans. All the rest are disguises, as are the claims to "justify" them, such as "Civil Rights, Affirmative Action, Reparations, Fairness, Equality, Progress" and the like.

How does communication effect such changes ? By _talking down_, a very potent force in our human psychology. Since we have no sensory organs for looking into ourselves, we are totally dependent and vulnerable to our view mirrored in the eyes of others. And this , ladies and gentlemen, has been the drumbeat directed at us by the "voices of society" since even before Columbia University taught their poison. I well remember reading of advice to young advertising students to visit Appallacian housewives to properly lower their level of address in copy-writing. THIS is what is taught and practiced, I claim, perhaps in more subtle form never-the -less, in contemporary "journalism". And it is why I and many others are "turned off" by "news", the "political process", participation in nascent protest movements, totally discouraged and disillusioned about our future. EXACTLY WHAT THEY WANT!

There were anti-Americans from the start of our country: they were called "T_ORY-ES_" then, loyalists to Britain, and this is what the Revolutionary War was all about. This conflict has been endemic from the beginning, Soros and his black puppet being merely the latest versions. Where do YOU stand ? With us, or against us ?

"NO !" - OUR ORIGINAL INDIVIDUAL DECLARATION OF INDEPENDENCE.

William S. Horowitz, M.D.
December 4, 2012

Do you remember our birth in life as a separate individual, a thinking and acting person, begins at age 2 with our first refusal of our mother's instruction? It is then that the basis for our development of a separate self and identity becomes possible. Then enabled to follow are the capacity to think, will, act, take initiative, make effort, sustain it for work, and accomplishment. Missing this step, all this development doesn't happen. Our origins, as eventual productive and collaborative citizens. arise in rebellion, which is echoed throughout early childhood, adolescence, and young adulthood by this same non-compliance.

The youth are by nature, and normally and healthily so, "left", politically. A youth lacking this adverse stance is headed for a life of abject passivity, a political "clone" to a charismatic leader, even less than a 3/5 constitutional person. Does a society of too many of these explain the apparent "stupidity" of our voters, a much greater factor in the apparent social decline we complain about? Can there be too much "conservatism", or compliance, for a healthy polity? I.e., can a society stagnate as well as explode, if these influences are out of balance?

After maturation, the adult is able to evaluate the claims of the two sides, make an informed decision.....based in part on an educated awareness of what has gone before.....and stand his ground in asserting it. He also demonstrates this strength and independence in his dealings with individuals in that society, often those in his personal society, his family.

A tree accumulates strength over seasons in its wood, whilst being receptive to contemporary influences in its leaves, all the while respecting its history in its roots. Do we emulate this in our development?

Is human nature changing?.... not likely. Is human society changing? ..... why not?..... every one in history has. Is the human prepared for this?.... not likely, the particular histories are all different. What is universally experienced is upheaval. no news to you.

SO, WHAT'S THE DIFFERENCE ?

William S. Horowitz, M.D.
February 4, 2013

No, this is not a rejoinder to Hillary's (in)famous wisecrack, her overt denial of a crisis, but an attempt to understand a puzzling phenomenon. We posed the question last time why humans seem to ignore differences between them and see instead identity. Of course we know the "politically correct" insistence on this for political purposes, but what are the human motives?

A succession of unhappy couples appear before Judge Judy. much too often of mixed races each partner having almost diametrically opposite views, values, expectations, and experiences....with no apparent recognition of the asymmetry of their relationship, either by them or their judge, who patiently tries to educate them into common sense whilst judiciously remaining silent about their disparity. This is a product of a modern social movement to encourage "diversity", one apparently avidly adopted by the modish masses.

Ralph Peters asserts regularly that this insistence flies in the face of human nature, which he claims historically has abjured racial mixing, people preferring to be with their own. For confirmation, visit any modern mixed college campus to view the spontaneous self-segregation which has taken place. So, are we seeing the ease of familiarity winning over the effort required of novelty? So, do we prefer to take those elements of sameness in the situation and ignore the differences? So, do we in effect perceptually convert diversity into identity for its comforting value? This makes a kind of half or partial relationship with a whole 'nother individual, half of each of them. That sounds like a weak commitment at best, which, if you watch Judy every day, begins to strike you as the near-universal case of modern marriage.

In these days of world-wide political unrest and threats of not only destruction of traditional social structures but even of our own very existence, ANXIETY is the keyword. THAT should favor arrangements that promote comfort, and indeed, it does if one looks under the covers. So, are we humans then reassuring ourselves in an era of rapid social change and threat that "nothing has really changed"? Did Hillary echo our own denial of crisis in her prescient words? Are we not saying the same: "So, what's the difference"? (There isn't any.)

MY ITCH

William S. Horowitz, M.D.
March 27, 2013
with Gloria's help

Lately I have been experiencing the strong urge to dig and peel off encrustations to expose what lies beneath. No, I am speaking of ideas; some surprising correlations have emerged in the inter-play of them.

We have learned from diverse sources that the typical form of government called democracy seems to have a short shelf-life down through the ages in the neighborhood of 200-250 years,. The mechanics are simple and straight-forward: unprotected mob-rule. It is the psychology of it we wish to explore further; what lies beneath.

We have posited that the idealistic founders, their heirs, and their tradition have died out in that time......to be replaced by whom ? Well, Sigmund taught us the most powerful rival to those fathers is called Oedipus, the son(s) who want to depose him. (To stay with describing the interplay of dynamic forces and leave real-life correlations to your research), the successor replacement father would likely guard against experiencing a similar fate by a re-enforced strong leadership which we call a dictator. When the ruled populace finally tires of the monotony, voicelessness, and lack of personal freedom, a rebellion might end the cycle to start a new one.

Now, here's a new idea: what would obviate the Oedipal rivalry of the sons against the father.....who doesn't have it? The daughter !!

Can a girl-child, enamored of her father and wishing an alliance with him become his heir ? Of course, and she could in effect become the non-rivalrous son. A likely identification with him could ensue, heretofore ascribed to "hormonal influences". Comfortable with the idea ? It's new and fresh and lies obscured beneath the crust of tradition. Perhaps this is beginning to resonate with some of you out there in real life....you can confirm later.

To continue, after a pleasant honeymoon between the two familial leaders, what would disturb the situation ?. Well, the old aforementioned forces, rivalry. From whom to whom? The siblings, now restless with irrelevance, the sons go after the daughter, convincing her she is as irrelevant as they and should leave the throne-room and stay in the kitchen. And there she has remained through history, until "The Movement". Her feeling of having been devalued seems quite appropriate, even when it comes to her assigned role as mother.

(It is true that recent history has witnessed the Western Queendoms of Victoria, Elizabeth. Beatrix, and Juliana, but the crucial evidence to be learned would be the experiences of Empresses like Cixi and Wu Zetian in the millenial stability of the Chinese government.)

So, the prideful and boastful (read "cocky) sons having prevailed over the father and the daughter(s) expend their remaining time in endless search for validation of their superiority....until someone from the masses who cares for them all rises to the heretofore height of statesman-leader, and the whole story repeats.

Not denying the significance of the psychological but re-affirming its necessity in the wider study of history, we need to also consider world events playing a major role in the fate of historical governments: wars, famines, disasters of various kinds, assassinations, the passage of time, preceding and simultaneous events, all must play a part. But it would really be an important contribution if any living female "sons" can tell us first hand the verity of our thesis. That would warrant a very important paper in its own right for the entire intelligent public to consider, not just the profession.

A PSYCHOLOGICAL LOOK AT SPECIES

William S. Horowitz, M.D.
March 25, 2013

The mammalians are species which breast feed their young, necessarily entailing caring for them, called mothering. Since this process extends over time, they, the mothers and the young, develop attachments to their fellow creatures which enables a social dimension to their society. On the other hand, the pre-mammalians have NO relationship to their young, which are dropped into this world to fend completely for themselves. They are reptilian, with all that connotation of viciousness, stealth, no society nor concern for its prey and fellow creatures alike (individuality).

Now, among the human members of the first group, there are further subdivisions or classes: mothers who feed from their warm bodies, those who feed cold/warmed milk from another species, those that give the young to feed on another, those that give their young away, those that choose not to have any, and those that destroy the ones they already grew. Not all those classes give rise to the same kind of society, as could be imagined, though out of empathy for our fellow-women, we tend to lump them all together. There are mothers, and then there are mothers.

Human society seems totally indebted to its mothers for its very existence, but they are as often honored as reviled for it. Does the emerging youngster need to feel he accomplished it all himself? Well, to separate from the social nexus, he feels the urge to develop a sense of self or individuality. Does that constitute a regression to an lower form? Or does it enable thinking (for himself)? Members of a group react and respond, reflexively; individuals ideate and initiate. Members of a group of mammals who are also individuals, that's human. Mammals which are not individuals are called sheep. Mammals who are individuals but not members of the group are called rogues.

What we are drawing a picture of is our diverse human society, contained within it both the highest and lowest development of living forms. With the passage of historical time, many groupings have arisen, among which the most influential have been the political and the religious. The drive to subdivide a diverse heterogeneous mass of people into some form of organization seems to be blended from both the need to socialize and to individuate.

Politics has been defined as the art of exercising power over people, used and abused by individuals, yes, but chiefly reflected in forms of government of their society. The most successful and long-lasting have been the dynasties or succession of dictatorial families. In order to avoid the tyranny of royal and other forms of endowed power, our Founding Fathers, wealthy, successful, responsible and mature individuals thought their country could be safely left to the guidance of men like themselves, hence self-rule was the philosophy chosen. Unfortunately they and their heirs and traditions died after two hundred years, replaced by considerably less virtuous populations which reverted to form. Today we have the perfect culmination of their democracy, rule by the demos or mob, with NO effective protection.. But, loyally, the members of the former group, the Chinese, are as proud of what they have developed over millennia as the members of the latter group, the Americans, who inherited their pride.

There is another manifestation of blind, irrational activity which is found in cult formation, wherein the personal charisma of a power-seeking individual draws unto himself a small group of easily enthralled individuals to share in his magic. Such groups either fall by the wayside over time, or eventually legitimize themselves by appeal to another kind of magic, that of unseen other-worldly phantoms, belief in which by means of intimidation, condemnation, and then redemption, wind up as organized religions and are actually worshipped as such !

What is the common denominator of these two historical phenomena? Job security for the politicians and the clergy, irrationality on our part. Is that because thinking is a relatively late individual development in us , because socializing came first ? Will humans do anything to belong? "Mother, don't leave me out !" I offer no definitive answers here, just random thoughts which hopefully will stimulate your thinking given some serious effort.

RESPECT

William S. Horowitz, M.D.
June 10, 2013

"I don't get no respect !", the plaintive plea of the woman since time immemorial. Familiar, yes ?.... to us all. Does it have some universal meaning, then ? Perhaps so....let us examine it.

The word respect has many meanings, such as honor, appreciation, evaluation, etc., but the most basic or primitive or first meaning is a common-sense grasp of physical superiority, by the weaker of the stronger. It is historically the source of the young child's attitude to the father, recognizing it's vulnerability to his displeasure. The child has no appreciation of his historic role in society, but perhaps does recognize that its mother seems to pay her respects to him, and one angry rebuke from him seals the wisdom of its doing the same.

Is the respect earned, legitimate, warranted? In the sense above, by all means, and the weaker one who is unmindful of it is in dire peril in this world. That has NO significance, however, in the higher appreciation of *respect,* which refers to qualities valued by our society. So, how does the child come by it? In the normal course of events in family life, it is nigh-on inevitable. But what in the AB-normal course of events.....say, no father ?

Aye, there's the rub, for increasingly in our society, there IS NO FATHER. Does such a child grow up lacking respect for fathers, or men in general ? Wouldn't bet against it. And how does the family get generated without a father? Well, sperms are available freely in this and every society, but committed fathers are definitely NOT. Especially by females, newly empowered or otherwise brave, who have decided THEY DON'T NEED ONE. And who are they? Perhaps children of fatherless families themselves, or THOSE THAT ASPIRE TO BE THE FATHER THEMSELVES. (Or, the leader, the number one, the stronger, the "star".) Those are the ones who plea for respect, for what the father has, what they don't have, when the womanly virtues of attractiveness, love, honor and the like don't seem to satisfy. They are the ones who want RESPECT!

Please note I haven't mentioned Sigmund once, but his insights have reached us all, universally, and it isn't really necessary....but I pay him my homage never-the-less, *my respects.* ! Think of all the sophisticates in academe and elsewhere who DON'T.....what do *they* reflect about father-less-ness? Is this a sad commentary on today's' now grown-ups?

What happens when such a woman marries a man who has grown up in a normal society with normal expectations? He feels relentlessly attacked by the woman who either fails to afford him respect or tries to take his "maleness" away? Are you really surprised to read DAILY of the murderous attacks on wives and girl-friends, whom they only wish to *LOVE?* There's another mystery solved, for you freshman sociologists out there. It's been my pleasure.

Daddy.

A SMALL HERITAGE

William S. Horowitz, M.D.
September 8, 2012

Five brothers in rural Georgia at the turn of the century, men with talent and ambition for commercial achievement, members of a Jewish family strictly minority status in that community, decide to adopt a new family name to enhance their acceptance, mull over current heroes of the extant society like Westinghouse, Carnegie, and Astor and finally choose Smith as their new moniker. Their old one remains unknown to their progeny. In later life, a Jewish woman whose family name still remains unknown, becomes a Smith by marriage to join the happy "Goyishe" family.

Fast forward to their grown daughter choosing marriage, with a Schmaltz, yet ! That marriage produces yet another daughter who within a short span of time is rendered a child of divorce. Her mother predictably re-marries a Jewish man with an Anglo-sized name, Jones for Josephson, and shortly forces the daughter to be adopted for "obvious convenience", so she. too, carries the new family name.

Still later in life she chooses yet another new husband, this time passing with a moniker suggestive of the British peerage. Does she know who she is, or was? Almost like she doesn't want to know. Her grandfather achieves great stature in the American society as a good (looking) Jew, and all 5 brothers achieve outstanding commercial success. But there isn't a Schmaltz or Josephson to be seen.

The aforementioned little girl with a brand new name, but no particular identification with that new family, grows up with a strange preoccupation: Who am I? (and a consequent inability to be open with people). Is it any wonder? If you are unfamiliar with the concept, I am describing a family of poseurs, from way back.

SOCIABILITY IS LIFE-ENABLING, ASOCIALNESS IS FATAL

William S. Horowitz, M.D.
December 18, 2012

When the human egg and sperm meet and "fertilize", they merge into one, the genetic strands unify themselves, then twist together as a random exchange of genes called amphimixis takes place, then the two original cells separate into two permanent composites of genes. This process is usually successful and will lead with cell development in time into a viable human being. But it is not always successful, with the result that the zygotes fail to develop, or do so but erratically, and eventuate into a fetus that spontaneously aborts, is still-born, or develops into a flawed new-born with a truncated life-span.

In the animal kingdom, we know that a new-born which does not interact with its mother is done for, but a human infant who on the very first day refuses to make eye-contact with its mother is gravely flawed, exhibiting the earliest signs of a-socialability, by whatever name we wish to call it. However we try to salvage such a human, its destiny is marked and we, the observing society, must reconcile ourselves to that reality.

There are degrees of resistance to relating to one's fellow humans, of course, but the quality is no different in the simple loner, the "autistic", the stealthy bomber, or the political war-monger, starvation meister, or outright mass-murderer, of which our past century had an abundance. That may have been the bloodiest century in history... if anyone really knows. There are also degrees of resistance to recognizing this gravity of anti-social manifestations, with our usual soft-hearted avoidance of hard-nosed policies which have given rise to eugenics and the "master race". What is so hard about recognizing that people who do not like their fellow social beings are killers, in mind and action? Seems like common sense.

Several handicaps come to mind which interfere with seeing clearly. Narcissism, or self-love doesn't see imperfection. Religious mythology, which values everyone as a creature of God's perfection. Pseudo-science, which develops a 'fix" for everything. A fuzzy infantile political philosophy of "equality" cannot differentiate. Very human compassion is pained and thus avoided. And so it goes. So, as usual, there are reasons why things are as they are. Doesn't mean they can't change.

TEAMWORK

William S. Horowitz, M.D.
April 13, 2013

Ever heard of it? Many young act as if they haven't heard, seen , practiced, or even knew of its existence.

In the "old days" we oldsters were all proud members of the team, honored to be accepted into it. I was a member of multiple "teams", and this was not at all unusual. It's why I assume you all automatically respond to the signals to participate in a team effort... and you don't......objecting, "No, YOU do it, let HIM do it".

My teams? The first was my family: with my father gone making a living, I was the only male at home to assume his responsibilities, and I did it with a proud sense of mission but careful not to abuse it and assume what was not mine. I remained the worker, not the captain. Then in school I joined the orchestra and played in it from 3 or 4th grade until graduating, ultimately winning the post of leader or concertmaster. I also joined the football team with a totally undistinguished record...but it felt GOOD.

Shortly after graduation with the country at war and with fuzzy personal prospects, I joined the military, the Naval V-12 program, which trained officers in the various professions: it was here I opted for pre-med. This program was finally disbanded after the war, but a call came for further service during "Korea", and I enlisted again in the Air Force, spending that war practicing in a team which evaluated "disabled" soldiers. With time on my hands, I volunteered to serve on the nightly OB service, in addition to learning golf, bridge, and serving on three bowling teams.

After the war, I pursued post-graduate medical training by joining the enthusiastic group fascinated with Freud's studies, which has remained my life work and adopted role model. Non-professionally I gathered a small group of colleague/friends to engage in regular meetings around investing, computer techniques, and the like, continued to this day. So, the "group" has remained my comfort, and I with sorrow anticipate the end of it.

My error, family. I'm from the old school.

THANK YOU, HELENE DEUTSCH

William S. Horowitz, M.D.
September 28, 2012

In 1934 she called our attention to a new patient phenomenon which she called the AS-IF Personality. She described their unanalyzability but offered no true dynamic explanation. I herewith present mine for your consideration, as well as a new diagnosis.

All of us have witnessed, nay, experienced the fascination a new human infant arouses in us. The intriguing thing is to speculate that this same infant, increasingly as he matures, experiences his random perceptions of his surrounding real world as fascinating, too.

It is as though this stage of development is marked by a quality of height perception, by both the viewer as well as the viewed. Sounds super-natural, doesn't it? But in our adult real world we have a name for something, an ineffable quality, which inures to certain people who fascinate us: charisma. Is this a later recognition, a re-edition, of the same thing?

What is the psychological medium that is being heightened? It is the perceptual function of attention. Our heightened atten-tion is drawn to the infant even as his is drawn to the multifarious objects in his surround. To make a leap to a somewhat (months) later development, the infant realizes he can capture the attention of his attendants, can manipulate them into action, can control them. This constitutes a definitive operation, function, phase, call it what you like, in the infant's first year of experience in this world: the manipu-lation of others' attention to control, possess them.

We loosely call it the young (Narcissist) drawing our attention, but it is much more complicated, powerful, and effective that that implies. It is a fixed phase of psychological functioning of the infant, tails off in ensuing years of development, hopefully to fully disappear in the well-functioning adult (except for what we allow to be called "normal narcissism")......BUT IS FIXED IN THE PROBAND WE CALL "AS-IF" OR CHARISMATIC CHARACTER.

In the psychoanalytic situation, absolutely everything the patient produces is an object of the analyst's scrutiny. It is a perfect medium for our subject to operate in, and he will, endlessly, for years even, without producing anything meaningful. That leads to the analyst's belated recognition that "nothing is happening" in the therapeutic situation and giving it up. When the proband realizes he has lost his effect and control, he leaves, his sole gratification having been eliminated. This is exactly the same as when the political observer says he cannot respond to Obama's mouthings because there is NOTHING in them. Our essay, therefore, has wide and profound implications, far beyond those of our parochial profession.

To this I wish to make every sentient citizen aware. Let us call it provisionally "Attentional Disorder" until a yet better term emerges.

THE FRAGILE "I"

William S. Horowitz, M.D.
February 26, 2013

Musing on the automatic disagreeableness of some people who, in reaction to proferred explanation or opinion by other people, take the opposite position and so seem unfriendly or overtly hostile. I was taken back to earlier theses I had advanced regarding left-handedness and general youthfulness, both of which sprung from the need to view from two separate "selves".

Now to explore the dynamic or energic conditions which make a "meeting of the minds" strenuously to be avoided. It starts with the 2 yr. olds first "NO" to his mother, which I have called his "Original Declaration of Independence." It is to be understood that he lived for two years as a fused "self" with her, only now feeling something separate on his own, probably bodily sensation in her absence, which he can even make happen !. This dawning awareness that "HE" exists is the start of a new mental representation of a "self", new, weak, untested as it is. It is easily lost, then regained in its nascent stages, as he experiments with it. It lacks the sturdiness and strength which it will gain with the passage of time, the repetition of making it happen, and the absence of untoward experience: (a mother NOT conducive to separation).

It is not hard to understand that "seeing it her way" subtracts from his own view, is felt as a loss of "self", and to the newly emboldened infant is UNWANTED. What may be harder to conceptualize is a walking-around adult who still feels that way !

BUT THEY DO ! Their "self", their "I", is not prepared to co-exist, co-llaborate, co-operate, consensualize, co-ANYTHING. It is "I", "ME", not you, at all times. We call our current generation the "ME" one, and observe it with a smile, knowing they will eventually grow out of it, no big harm done.

Two important issues need to be introduced now. The first has been covered numerous times as the biological principle of unity. Nature does NOT make two of every creature, only ONE. The apparent two-ness derives from the existence of a young form and it's mature end-stage, its adult. There are a variety of life forms to be sure, lions and tigers, e.g., but they are variations of the same thing, what we call a family. The same with the two genders, variations of the same thing.

We are NOT born alone; we come into existence as part of a family, we are a social creature just like monkeys and elephants, and we do NOT think, feel, act as "individuals"; and those that do we call rogues and misfits and relegate them to the criminal class (their family). Talk about unity, did you know that ALL of Mother Nature's creatures share the identical inheritance mechanism ?

Where do we get the idea of two-ness? It is an artificial construct of the legal mind, which operates on conflict, argumentation. And that's who wrote the constitution: the lawyers, so that the legislators could debate, argue, hopefully to reach a consensus. That would be the rationale, but in fact it only guaranteed perpetual employment. The Congress is a debating society, not an action committee. And that is why there is no mention of the family, the social unit of the society. in our founding document. Our thinking has been corrupted by lawyers: it is NOT reality. If you are seeking a statesman working for the benefit of the whole nation, look no further than the generals who led us into and out of war: Washington, Lincoln, Eisenhower !

The other issue is what has enabled the young to prevail politically, the granting them an equal voice and privilege to the adults. Nowhere else in nature does this arrangement exist, being so obviously unnatural. The young are treasured, protected, nurtured, but not granted social power until they earn it by becoming acquainted with the way things are, which we call maturing, which just happens with the passage of untrammeled time. To grant them political power prematurely is to SPOIL them.

What we fail to realize is that we are observing the genesis of a powerful political movement: the youth, the radicals, the left, the progressives, and the liberals which have actual sway over us.

Their "eventuality" is extremely long-term, and holds no prospect of "growing up" any time soon. We tolerate them, as misbeguided children, or co-equal sides of the polity, or threats to our existence...... but we mature adults, conservatives, rightists, Independents seem mis-matched in our public voice. Do we not take them seriously enough, are their radical attacks trivialized, do we "tolerate" them in good Christian and American tradition, DO WE REALIZE OUR COUNRY COULD BE LOST TO THEM?

Grown-up Americans, WAKE UP, your country is being taken over by spoiled children. And Vox Populi, "democracy", good luck, and past history are no assurances of a favorable outcome: the "family" of separate states may need to be the effective corrective agency.

THE GESTURE

William S. Horowitz, M.D.
July 31st, 2010

What does the bride and groom do when wedded? What does the principal and graduate do? What does the President do with the child with outstretched arms? What does the mother do to the returning prodigal son? What do the young lovers do espying each other from a distance and approaching? What does the newborn infant and mother do? What does the little monkey, also by instinct, do?

They all embrace, they HUG, the universal inborn automatic primate centripetal reaction to the other. It may or may not be consummated with a kiss, a second-level apposition of intimacy, denoting and communicating yielding to the urge to merge. Thus we betray our underlying human history of having been one and the magnetism still extant in it.

We even have in our armamentarium the anti-hug, the middle-finger or forearm salute, the off-fending push, the rebuke, the barb, the needle, the provocative remark designed to make distance. And, gentlemen as we are, we have the polite intermediate greeting of the handshake, which also can be warm or cool; not too close, not too distant.

Whence cometh this array of human gestures toward each other? We take these for granted, so in-grained are they in our experience, but they didn't arise from nowhere, nicht wahr? Where did they come from? They are derived, I submit, from the earliest inter-human physical contact in all our experiences, from the mother-infant one we all went through.

Can they be understood as social developments over time as the individual matures and has different greeting intentions to express? Undoubtedly. But can they be understood in yet a different way, reflecting perhaps the nature or character of the original holding experience between different kinds of mothers and different kinds of infants? Can these be of different degrees of warmth and coldness? Can different humans have different degrees of comfort with interpersonal distance? Sociologists have long noted the pattern in this dimension in different geographical (read temperature), social, and religious groups, and now we psychologists should add personality or temperament.

What a fine distinction we are drawing here, but what a consequential one for human life experience! It's importance cannot be over- weighted. How many friendships or even marriages have foundered on such a disharmony between partners, how many individuals have been attracted or repelled by the comfort level in certain social, religious, or political groups? How many have even felt alienated from or belonging to the whole human race?

Just one more thing to ponder in the realm of discrimination of differences.

THE MAN SEEKS, THE WOMAN NESTS

**William
and Gloria Horowitz,
her birthday gift to us.
April 20, 2013**

"The way things were?" NO, the way things are! The little boy jumps on his bike to go...anywhere. The little girl sits on the floor playing house with her dollies. It has been ever so in our times, and most will instantly recognize it: "the way we ARE."

The grown up woman is content to have her very own real family, and raising her children and husband provides all the gratification she seeks. There are always opportunities to raise other things, her garden, other children if a school teacher, healing sick patients if a caretaker, educating the public if a writer, et cetera. Can she fly a plane, compete on an athletic team, contribute sociological insights like these? Of course....and likely at the same time as she comes home to make dinner for her family. (our author is doing just that !) Exercising the woman's' capacities gives her the satisfaction of being competent, which in turn enriches and strengthens her society and its economy.

The grown up married man goes OUT everyday to his work, seeking advancement in that work, doing more business, making more money, discovering more secrets as an inventor or scientist, et cetera.

Can he play in a symphony, write a novel, compete in a track meet ?... Of course he can, but likely comes home each evening with the "bacon" to join the comfort of his family. And he feels fulfilled and accomplished, having a place in society, belonging.

Are you laying down a rule, a generalization, a flat dictum ? What of the exceptions, the outliers from the norms? Granted, our society these days is providing for all kinds of exceptions (cf. transgender operations), but the question is why ? Has it deviated so far from the norm that it no longer recognizes it....Is it unwilling to deal with the way things are, with reality?

We weren't there and can only imagine what it was like in pre-history when life was "short and brutish". The realities of existence must have carried an immediacy of impact that left little room for dreaming, though we know humans did wonder about causes and imagined powerful unseen forces controlled events. So, fanciful ideas have been around from the beginning and undoubtedly had a powerful influence....(cf. human sacrifice to the "Gods")....but the exigencies of survival had their own primacy and necessity and ignoring them was fatal. Today we seem less controlled by fact, freer to imagine....is easier survival making us more susceptible to fables, fancy, and foolishness ?

Many in our modern society seem to believe they are dealing with an advanced understanding of reality....progressive and up-to-date. They see "conservatives" as "flat earth" types, stuck in the past, succeeding in turning the discussion on its head, rendering convention passe and themselves in the vanguard. If there were a genuine philosophic debate that would be one thing, but in actuality, "left-liberal" thinking is the misguided fanciful imagination we historically mocked. It covers and disguises a naked cynical political ploy to win popularity, votes and money to keep themselves in power. Today we pursue "smart" ideas like preserving the snail darter or spotted owl in the face of astronomically rising unemployment, debt, plus incidents of a revived historic religious war being actively waged worldwide.

What is the point of all this? Historians tell us that past eras have seen the accepted understanding of certain subjects being totally forgotten over time until re-discovered anew, almost a cyclical evolution in human knowledge. Are we in a declining slide toward ignorance in the face of so much amassed modern knowledge? Are we regressing in the name of progressing ?

Those that espouse the conventional view, the "conservative" perspective on how things are, not numerically but at least politically, in the minority in our society, compared with those who prefer to operate on the way things ought to be....(In the study of dreams we call it wish-fulfillment). To use a contemporary term, the narrative has changed....some will say captured or high-jacked....with the effect that today, with endless unemployment compensation and Government support for single mothers and freely-available abortion, many men have given up seeking, women nesting. Is that better? The empowerment of the populace and its society is in sharp decline, while the controlling class doesn't seem to care, or worse.

THE PETER PAN SYNDROME

William S. Horowitz, M. D.
February 22, 2013

Who was Peter Pan? He was a fictional character in a turn of the century novel by J.M. Barrie, who modeled him after his real brother who died at 14 and remained at that age in his mother's mind. We refer to him as the boy who never grew up. What does his syndrome refer to? To actual living people (in America more likely a girl-child) who seem to exercise a moratorium on maturing, as though they have been granted a pass on this universal responsibility. Being well aware of others' aging, they don't want to, and feeling themselves an exception, don't have to. And that is the hallmark of the symptom complex: the stubborn avoidance of responsibility, ultimately for the self.

One of the main causative agents is fear, perhaps the predominant one, from a variety of circumstances which left the child feeling a lack of both inner resources and external protection, thus doubly vulnerable, thus fearful. This marks the psychic state as phobic, from inexperience. A supplementary cause is having been given a pass from childhood responsibilities by the parent, often by indulgence.

Since he is not doing anything, nor has done anything, all influences seem as originating from the outside, rendering a picture easily passed for as paranoid. Also, because he has done nothing, he feels blameless, beyond any criticism, ideal, perfect, all arrogantly proclaimed, a model to be esteemed (and a victim to be pitied). Those others not so favored are seen as deficient, less than himself, but there is constant measuring and comparison taking place, rendering the picture of rivalry and envy (of him and of them, who have achieved what he hasn't).

He deals in semi-versions of reality, with ample doses of fantasy, wishful-thinking, make-believe, the whole viewed as a magical world. Time, money, death, other aspects of reality are only partially grasped. NO WONDER he DOES NOT want to hear certain things, to learn what really happens out there, to become knowledgeable, to become educated. And, furthermore, who knows more to teach him? The only prospect is that of becoming even more disillusioned. Better to wrap himself in the comforter of ignorance and belief (as well as the self-satisfaction of already knowing it all).

This works well in actual childhood and youth, but the rub comes in as an adult, because the brain continues to develop while the mind remains idled. Then he is in turmoil, recipient of frightening mixed messages from his smarts and dumbs, both. The other hurdle is being confronted with the necessity to assume (older) adult responsibilities after a relatively effortless sojourn amongst his children. Those conflicts can add to the motivation to re-regress, or in the rare case of effective countermeasures, to overcome the pause and continue development. It is, after all, a dynamically motivated conflicted psychic state which can be unraveled, not an organic permanent flaw. But I imagine to the subject, its undoing is a world-shaking event with uproarious protests to match.

What are the outward characteristics of Peter? A youthful unwrinkled countenance, even as he ages, a fascination with things of youth such as toys, dolls and animals. Because he feels as one of them, his care of children (and needful adults) is unparalleled in focus, concern and passion, almost super-human. Simple rather than sophisticated dress, interest in primitive societies, trivial or simplified translations of complex phenomena offered him, stubborn resistance to his view being challenged, argumentativeness, altogether feeling insulted at his perfect state (read authenticity) being questioned, and a background feeling of guilt for his forgone responsibilities. What really flabbergasts him is the apparent kid-glove or walking on egg-shell tolerance of his "difference" by his family finally giving way to exasperated IN-tolerance when all patience is lost with his pose. (That is a technical problem for those dealing with him, not his.)

Perhaps his outstanding trait is his very difference from other, usual people. That can be idealized into something rare and beautiful to behold, an ageless child, but it is NOT NORMAL, and that finally makes its appearance during the exigencies of adult life when higher functioning is called upon. And now the kicker: although this essay has been couched in the male gender, it is actually prototypical of some females in our society, delineating how she is excused from burdens borne by the male, how she is frequently granted a moratorium on assuming responsibility, "spoiled" if you will, contributing in part to her secondary social role and perceived by her as weakness, incapacity, and unfairness, which is what is rebelled against by the "feminists".

THE SINS OF THE FATHER(S)....

William S. Horowitz, M.D.
February 16, 2013
Thanks to Shirley Horowitz Rinder

Humans, like their monkey ancestors, are social creatures, meaning the bonds between individuals and their groups are essential and a source of comfort and feeling of well-being, and when broken, insecurity. When an individual feels no longer a member of his group, he feels like an outsider, not belonging, black sheep, rogue, which we call alienated. What can give rise to this feeling? Any breach of a social compact or custom or value of the group can rupture the good feelings between people and cause the subject to feel and be rejected. Any significant difference; whether meritorious or degrading makes no difference: it is the loss of harmony or together-ness between them that does.

What alienates humans from their group (read FAMILY) ? Serious sources include any fracture of customary arrangements such as abortion, divorce, co-habitation, single mother, popular bi-racial coupling, premature conception, marked disparity between parents in religious beliefs, intelligence, values, education, social standing, tradition, etc. Also departure from normative behavior such as criminality, drug use, contraction of a social disease, loss of public reputation, etc. But by far the greatest "sin" in the book is LEAVING the group, for which an automatic sentence of rejection is imposed. What does that say for our mobile society?

There is an identifiable character to geographic areas of our (or any) country, such as The East, The South, The Midwest, the Far West, The Northwest, and then there's California, the land of the "Fruits and Nuts" (not so inappropriate). Except for the native born, almost everyone there has come from someplace else, and in our definition, is alienated from his original group. Rootless, adrift, no wonder he becomes radicalized politically and socially, far left, faddish, exaggerated, and dealing in phantasy (unreal). Any move, between areas or whole countries, entails "leaving home" and its roots.

It's not just geography: the child of divorced parents is injected into a new family of a complete stranger, plus possibly losing the relationship with one of his parents: completely out of it. Thus begins the generational passage of seven. Likewise for the migrant, the hybrid believer, the mixed race child, and other worshippers of diversity. Succeeding generations confront succeeding strange-ness until familiarity finally takes place. The biological "natural" family contains all the variety and heterogeneity necessary and compatible with healthy development, requiring no improvement.

What is the point, then, of tracing the vicissitudes of alienation? To return to the theme of the signal importance of family in human affairs, the unit of organization of our society. NOT INDIVIDU-ALS, as many would say, but families of individuals make up our polity...but I don't think that term is mentioned in our Constitution.

TO BELONG

William S. Horowitz, M.D.
January 12-18, 2013

Two British Classic films recently repeated the observation that their society honored tradition, what WAS, while America looked to what WILL BE. This is a profound and far-reaching distinction, reflecting as it does stability and constancy vs. expansion and lability. To the extent that this characterization is true, what does it illuminate about ours ?

Without a class-defined society, do our people doubt they belong? Does our excess of father-less-ness, (our prime suppliers of legitimacy), further exacerbate the insecurity of our children? Does this unconnected-ness lead to excessive mobility in the society, with a major migration to the "new-er" land, the West and California? Does this resulting root-less-ness lead to a kind of disorientation called anomie? Does this, in turn, lead to radical political thought and weakening of traditional values (immorality)?

We welcomed whole peoples to the "New World" for its promise of exceptional dream-fulfillment Did this attraction, which eventually led to polyglot overcrowding, wear out its promise so that the dream became an ironic immigrant nightmare? Did the resultant un-unified and un-identified society lack the cohesive force of its founding spirit and tradition so that its functioning no longer worked efficiently? Power-seeking and corruption replaced governmental supervision, legislative effectiveness, the constitutional provision for balance of powers, the justice system, all deteriorated. Not to mention overt attacks to defeat our nation. And the built-in provisions for correction no longer prevailed.

We have all heard that Democracies have a self-limited shelf-life of 250 years because they are unprotected (from their own). Is this precisely what we are witnessing now, we American veterans of the Great Depression and two World Wars, imbued since our origins in the magnificence of our beloved Red, White & Blue? For the first time in our lives, WE are thinking of going to live somewhere else. We don't feel we belong anymore.

TOUCH

William S. Horowitz, M. D.
June 14th, 2013

Kitty's Birthday
Gloria's Observations

A profound subject has been opened to me today, and I am impelled to put my thoughts down in this paper. It is highly personal, yes, but I hope has relevance to other members of my family, and beyond.

Humans are social creatures requiring the company of others of their kind. What is the medium of contact with those others? I propose it is the _ectoderm,_ the fetus's outer embryonic layer, which includes prominently the skin, but also the perceptual apparatuses and the brain. We make _contact_ with each other through these tissues and organs. Brain ideas presented here hopefully will touch you and thus have impact.

My wife, a critical if not dispassionate observer of my behavior for 40 years, calls me a "Yo-Yo" man, blowing hot and cold in turn regarding my relationships to others. She sees me as alternately pushing away and then drawing close with her and others, maybe like what lovers do, and perhaps people in general. She developed her cool and over-looking powers of observation from the back seat of the family automobile as a then-single child, as her parents travelled the nation appearing often obliviously embroiled in a passionate love-affair. This followed a lonely childhood in her all-adult family's greenhouse.

Now to introduce more specifics, I was raised by a mother who experienced what we now call PTSD, having been run over by a horse which permanently scarred her, then separated from her large family to be raised alone by her Grandmother. SHE, for sure, was a Yo-Yo person, my sister and I agreeing she was in contact with us for only seven minutes before breaking it off to retreat to the mirror to refresh her self image. That was her capacity for human contact, it appeared, and we, the rest of the family adapted and otherwise identified with it. I think I am a product of that developmental experience, as my wife was with hers.

My body is covered with small black crusts, so uncomfortable that I spend my spare time _peeling_ them off to expose fresh skin. That feels _wonderful,_ but an observer has mistaken it for self-mutilation. ! Other channels of contact are impaired from old age, including hearing, eyesight, and memory-loss of normal vocabulary, but _fortunately,_ my writing still seems to come to me, and I retreat to it many sleepless nights. This essay illustrates well both my need to reveal myself, and to "look into".

My father was a _"travellin' man",_ a hard-working volatile, passionate veteran of the wars, who typically spent one weekend out of every two to six weeks to have his car washed and enjoy some "home _cookin"_ . During this time, MY parents made their frustrations known to all and indiscriminately, familiarly. We were relieved when he returned to the road, sad to say, but he kept working at whatever he could find and supported us so that we could reside in an upscale suburb (with WPA help). The superb school system there, insisted upon by my aspirational mother, was and still is my savior ! I kept in touch with my elementary school "gang" for 50 years, ultimately replaced by organizing an "investment club" of colleagues, still meeting 35 years later.

Now, for the _other critical_ history. My father suffered from severe body-covering red plaques, identified by the Navy as _PSORIASIS,_ the treatment of which necessitated a year's hospitalization in Texas, and of course follow-up home treatments, especially oatmeal baths. (Interestingly, when his children finally left home, he returned to live full-time with my mother and they went into business together, whereupon his disease became a minor one.) My sister and I suffer from larval forms of this very same disability. The question in my mind after living with this for 88 years, is it _"inherited ?_ Or is it _"Induced"?_ Think about it ! A coincidence, or a _"psychosomatic"_ effect? The pathologic changes in Psoriasis amount to making normal skin into _THICK SKIN !_ Implications ?

People obviously have varying needs for both isolation and contact, that is self-evident. But do we, perhaps, have our own individual rhythms of alternation between them while expressing our requirement for "self-preservation"? To toss in some additional facts for possible relevance to this thesis, I have married 4 times, (the longest 32 years dissolved by death), my sister 3. Her "*forme fruste*" of psoriasis is less extensive than mine. My daughter, raised in a broken home as an infant, has located herself in Northern California and taken up the profession of "Therapeutic Touch, Ala Rosen". My son, after a 4 year live-in with a woman he was preparing to marry but was refused, spent the next decade sleeping between two brute dogs. My wife, unable to leave her sanctuary cottage of a half-century, experiences *each day* the need to seek "fresh air" outside.

Which re-minds us the urge to touch and be touched is a central aspect of sexuality, but the obverse is not necessarily so. For instance, the freedom to disregard life-long conventions that comes with age, the weakening of other channels of contact, and the defocussing of local erotic zones to spread over the whole body....all may combine to result in a familiar problem for care-takers of the elderly and senile: their tendency to *take their clothes off*! And maybe related, what about the end-of-life attraction to "reveal it all" intellectually?... to write an autobiography? Am I doing that here, in addition to "Looking into"?

There are other pathologies of touch, such as diabetic neuropathy and the character disorder of <u>NARCISSISM</u>, but perhaps this brief excursion will have piqued your interest to ponder further yourselves. I have attempted to sketch here one man's family history of the vicissitudes of their "contact" drive. For what it is worth, my wife and I agree we were essentially untouched growing up, left to our own devices as good, compliant, "no-trouble" kids essentially being their own parent to themselves.

What would we ever do without our *monkey* inheritance?

VOCABULARY LESSON

William S. Horowitz, M.D.
16 July, 2012

Do you know what a SINECURE is? The slang definition is "cinch" or "snap". The more formal definition is a guaranteed undemanding job and pension for life ! Did your high school teacher tell you that she had one? Did your college instructor profess his secure position? Did you newly elected representative, or your career senator tell you why his position is sought and fought after? Ever heard the song, "Everybody's doin' it?"

Why the lowly citizen or even non- is being provided for in this kingly fashion to preserve his vote. It seems the order of the day in this young democracy, after 200+ years of building a productive society that was the protector and envy of the rest of the world.

Our so-called "founding fathers" were wealthy land and slave owners who, in their security fashioned a governing arrangement to be populated and run by mature and secure adults like themselves. They referred to them as citizens, operators and caretakers of the nascent society. They envisioned that the menace to former nations came from above, the inherited class. They assumed the "struggling masses" would be delighted at the chance to improve their lot, and indeed it was so as the rush to populate the empty land continued..... to....when?

Cynics observe democracies last until their people discover they can vote themselves the Treasury. Is this what we have come to? We hear complaints about the do-nothing Congress, and when will the "adults" there wake up and do something ?!! Well, they've already awakened to how their bread is buttered and done something. We hear complaints about the "take" society, but why should they do any different ? So then we are left with the rest of us, watching and waiting for the "Power of the People" to assert itself. Well, who will step forward and cast the first stone?

Are we in the process of circling back to the beginning, where that aphorism had cogency? Are we awaiting a savior?

Do ordinary people have the capacity to govern themselves, as we were led to believe.? Or, have we bought into a pipe dream? There is no doubt we are disillusioned? Is there help?

Rare ordinary men, sensing both the danger and the opportunity, have on occasion risen to the obvious need and done the deed, and been honored for their nobility, sadly too often postmortem. But history is more often a tale of ignoble men satisfying a private grievance and doing great damage by the same deed. Be careful what you wish for.

WHAT DO MEN WANT?

February 2013

Original Contribution by Gloria:

Freud is known for having pondered the question "what do women want"?.....I am pondering the question of "what do men want"?

In observations I have made of men over my lifetime, they seem to always be seeking something (else)... a "new" woman (perhaps the elusive perfect mother?)....she would make me happy, understand my needs; the current woman is lacking (what?)....a new powerful red sports car (masculinity)....more land (substantial)....seek at the top of the mountain, seek at the bottom of the ocean....in California, I will find what I am seeking....maybe Europe would satisfy me.....a small proportion of men, however, seek out the couch and the television preferring only to observe how other men seek out their fantasies....

This "new" woman hasn't worked out either, but I have another in mind....she is "perfect" for me....finally bliss.....I was wrong, a black town car with tinted windows (dignified/powerful) is what I need.....and my house, I need to be living higher on a hill (respect)....

I do not have enough land....I shall have to go to WAR....I will take what I need around the world....they can't stop me....I will seek and make weapons they can't even imagine....

My new woman has turned out to be a good wife, but now just a wife.....I am bored....I find the maid exciting and inviting.....what does my wife understand about this....after all, I'm just a man....I can't help it if my needs aren't being met; it's her fault....I will keep seeking until my needs are met.....

Maybe I should be an investment consultant....all that money these rich people have....I will seek and take what I need of it....

However, the world would not have moved forward without this "trait" of man, this seeking always and forever....they are driven creatures, but what drives the man?

Too long a story to tell of the men who are "driven" to make our lives longer and hopefully better....seeking new drugs, new hearts, new limbs....seeking to even find the answers in our soul, breaking through to the secrets that make us us.....and finally they will seek to make clones....the ability to make for us a "new" copy of our loved ones who are leaving the earth....never having to grieve again....

What does man have that woman does not.....male hormones, male wiring, imagination, sexual conquest/programmed orders from above to populate the earth, adventure, risk, a desire for dominance over all as promised in the Bible?......

Whether a man is creating a project in his basement, is in a nuclear submarine under the North Pole or in a spaceship en route to the moon, he is seeking satisfaction and only finding it temporarily.....what would mankind be without this dissatisfaction?.....why does the man cross the road?

Tell me, Sigmund, what do men want?

WHAT HATH GOD WROUGHT?

William S. Horowitz, M.D.
March 1st, 2013

The Negro slaves of Africa were captured and sold for money by Arab and Negro slave masters, transported and sold again for money to an international market including America, where they were paid for by southern farmers into conditions where at least they could stay alive (for the most part) and work off their indebtedness. Came the inevitable revulsion at the practice, millions of American citizens gave their lives in battle for their freeing, and the newly liberated or escaped slaves showed their gratitude by also fighting for the free-ers. Those slaves now enjoyed full citizen rights in a (semi) modern society and avidly accepted and "enjoyed" those rights, grateful to a man never to have to return to their "homeland".

That the American society was slow to fully accept them as "equals" (same) was wholly human and natural, and did nothing to detract from the credit Americans were due for their compassionately righteous deed. Fast forward to present day and witness how the whole situation has been completely turned on its head by a coterie (black) of social gamers and manipulators, to "work" the American psyche into a state of totally unjustified guilt, to where the rescued are now due reparations, special treatment, access to government for the regular and free exercise of theft, and a large proportion of them have reverted to animal savagery, crime, and mayhem. And another coterie (white) of gamers have seized the opportunity to amass votes for their own political power in the name of the "poor unfortunates" while doing nothing to actually improve their lot.

What started out as a collection of religious and political refugees, largely Christian, asserting their God-given right to self-determination in a new, rich, distant land...this brave assertion of wholesome righteousness...shortly fell victim to UN-Godly venality, initially practiced by depredations on the native population of the new land. How are we to hold in our heads the co-existence of high-minded ideals and the simultaneous presence of venal acts? Is this mankind, is this the doing of the Deity?

How is one to know? What do we tell our young?

The demography of the black (yes, NEGRO) race (yes, RACE) has been given as somewhere between 10 and 15 % of the American population, whilst the average American T-V viewer would not be mistaken to estimate it at least 50 % ! I, for one, am tired of having an omnipresent black face being pushed into my face, as well as being asked to observe polite false names for what we are dealing with. This is all a part of the synthetic, false, unreal existence we are experiencing, to our utter confusion and nowhere-ness.

I HAVE HAD IT, and hereby declare my independence from posture. We can call it a new 60's FREE SPEECH movement if it resonates with you. Try saying and writing the REAL words.

WHO KNOWS ?

(A companion to "NO")
William S. Horowitz, M.D.
December 14, 2012

What the 2 yr. old gains in his separation from mother, freedom to act on his own, he loses in knowledge of the world. He himself doesn't know "nuttin'", and embarks on a life-long search for someone who does. THIS may provide the motive for a RE-union with the missing authority. We recognize and fear our ignorance, but we believe someone else knows what we don't. Hence, we are drawn to the teacher, the preacher, the expert, the guru, the rabbi, the pope, the "GOD", and their system of belief for our security. They KNOW! (All of them M_ _ _ _ _ in disguise.)

Our socially-acceptable institutions such as school, religion, schools of philosophy and political parties may not be fundamentally different from a CULT , a gathering around a person or group who offers the security of those who KNOW. The intriguing thing is that theories of scientific discovery can promise the very same attraction... as any other belief system... and held to by the same terrified grasp.

We follow our favorite climatologist in the desperate belief that he KNOWS, and he, in turn, clings to the theoretical model HE was taught by HIS guru. This is only one of a multitude of "scientific" fads which have arisen over time, around all of the vital concerns of the human race. (Think your own list.) Now, consider that we consult a "mind expert" to figure out what we are thinking... is this any different? Is Psychiatry a science? Ask one. Is Psychoanalysis a science? Have we "bought into" the comforting trust that it is... or might it be a belief system invented by the Americans who discovered Freud and made his novel discoveries into a semi-religious practice for their own comfort ?

(How does it happen that such a practice can exhibit wild enthusiasm and then total disrepute in less than 50 years?)

This raises the question whether many, most, all our "scientific" knowledge is just a belief system... well, the "creationists" will gladly agree... except theirs may be, too. Well, what do we know for sure ? What does anybody know ? Who knows? There is a group that doesn't ask that question, is seeming not to search for ultimate knowledge... we call them A theists... those that don't believe. They seem confident in their own knowledge and ability to learn what more is needed. They seem fully developed, mature adults... but our society of believers scorn them. Then there are the disillusioned, those who have lost their belief but desperately seek some shard of meaning in something, absent which they are ready to give it all up; we call them agnostics or skeptics (or 1/2 believers ala Mencken) .

Then there are the animals... do they seek ultimate knowledge? Not so's you can tell... they seem content to know, after they learn, what they need to know to survive. Are WE, then, the seekers, the believers, attempting to achieve the prerogative of the Allmighty from our humble station? We are not given to know it all, and we don't need to know it all... are we just exhibiting our vanity (and fear)?

WHO WAS HETTY GREEN ?

William S. Horowitz, M.D.
February 9, 2013

This is an example of a long-distance entirely speculative analysis of an historical figure, aspects of which I hope you may learn from.

She was a prototype of someone we read about in the papers from time to time who is discovered to be a reclusive millionaire living in squalor, her house choking on her hoarded collections. How does this happen? We will attempt a possible dynamic sketch of such a person; it is NOT an actual biography of her.

More often she is an aging female, but not necessarily, living in a cosmopolitan setting by herself, with perhaps some cats but no friends or family. She is a miser, accumulating for a lifetime things of value or not, giving away nothing, especially money (no will). She is frugal in her habits: dress, food, quarters, and their maintenance. She is intelligent, having amassed a fortune, but modest and soft-spoken about what she knows, giving the impression of faux stupidity, and not above trying to make you feel so. Being bright and curious but demeaning of what the teacher knows, she is ambivalent about learning and thus uneducated or an autodidact. Altogether, she seems a simultaneous winner and loser in the social competition of life. And this provides the clue to her motivation.

She is consumed with envy, the feeling she has less, that others have more, which she covets. Social class, money, station in life, knowledge, love, and any of the values that can be measured, compared, and competed for are keenly felt as short. Hence, she accumulates what she can acquire and hoards it, giving nothing away, and hides and disguises what she does have to avert the envy of others toward her. No boasting or advertising, a very low profile and matching self-regard. And she devalues others, showing disdain and contempt for what they have. In addition, if they offer to give to her,

119

she spitefully refuses to acknowledge it, denies its value, argues for an alternate (better) view.

Giving no or minimal credit to them, she exhibits no gratitude for any assistance she has received, altogether feels she is a self-made person. This (ambivalently) expanded self-regard is allergically sensitive to criticism and completely intolerant of it, as though something is taken from her. A feeling of perfection, idealism, superiority marks her "ego", right alongside its simultaneous opposite of feeling worthless (winner and loser, remember?). She appears locked into a dead end with no future....hence she is ever contemplating death and its forerunner, illness ⟶ hypochondriasis.

Genesis? She may have been an entirely normal person to begin with before the exigencies of life dealt her blows, perhaps excessively, repeatedly. What could account for the source of her all-consuming envy? The underlying cause might have been a chronic deprivation, emotional or material it doesn't matter, yielding an embittered sustained resentment, "a bad taste in her mouth", at having been cheated out of her just due. But the additional aggravating factor may lie here: recall there are multiple rivalries in our communal life, but perhaps the original resides in the family (remember Oedipus ?), and in that family the most obvious is sibling rivalry. And perhaps the others are gender rivalry, right along with age rivalry and size rivalry (from birth order: being smallest).

Connecting those four sets of dots, is there a possible older brother in the picture? And if that envied rival whom she wished eliminated should have died.....(after others, yet)? Can you imagine the guilt over that "omnipotent" wish, the resultant depowering of the self, the phobic avoidance of asserting anything? If so, you are picturing the possible psychology of such a lost soul, for whom our hearts go out in sympathy.

Remember, this is a hypothetical construction for its instructive value only.

We have no Hetty Green here, but if she were, she would be capable of understanding what had happened to her, and that could help. That is the rationale of psychoanalysis.

www.ingramcontent.com/pod-product-compliance
Lightning Source LLC
Chambersburg PA
CBHW070708290526
45790CB00001B/496